Islands in the Wind

The political economy of the English East Caribbean

CLAUDE M. JONNARD

iUniverse, Inc.
New York Bloomington

iUniverse books may be ordered through booksellers or by contacting:

iUniverse
1663 Liberty Drive
Bloomington, IN 47403
www.iuniverse.com
1-800-Authors (1-800-288-4677)

Because of the dynamic nature of the Internet, any Web addresses or links contained in this book may have changed since publication and may no longer be valid. The views expressed in this work are solely those of the author and do not necessarily reflect the views of the publisher, and the publisher hereby disclaims any responsibility for them.

ISBN: 978-1-4401-9426-9 (sc)
ISBN: 978-1-4401-9427-6 (ebook)

Printed in the United States of America

iUniverse rev. date: 11/19/2009

This book is dedicated to my family and friends,
colleagues and students,
And to
MONTSERRAT
Emerald of the Caribbean

Contents

1

Personal Recollections

I- A long time ago

When I was young, I took a trip to the West Indies to fulfill a childhood dream. I was in my late teens; I was bored and curious; and it seemed to be the right thing to do at the right time. I visited a school friend who moved to Miami and within days the city became a staging area for my plan to spend the summer making the rounds of the big and small islands of the Caribbean.

Miami was a scruffy, gritty seaport in those days and it also had an airport. Freighters and small, island hopping planes routinely puddle jumped from one island to the next with manufactured goods, returning with sugar, rum and bananas. I was underway on a new adventure within days.

If I must behold my adult life as an enduring adventure that has yet to end and need to find its beginning, it may have been that summer. It was not that I took things seriously and planned for the future. Returning in September to get on with my life, I buried the memories of that trip in the scrapbook of my mind. I completed my education, joined the Army, found a job, got married and raised a family. And yet, my first job was in the import-export business, and I have stayed in the arena of international trade ever since as a professor of economics and finance and owner-operator of an export firm. It may have therefore been more than a passing coincidence that I ended up specializing in the emerging markets of the English speaking eastern Caribbean, those same islands where I spent so much time that summer a long time ago.

It is fair to state that the allure of the islands hooked me like an addict and when I was not traveling on business I was taking my family to one or more vacation Caribbean destinations at least once or twice a year. Looking back, it must have started with that childhood fascination with the Caribbean when I read books and saw movies about pirates that made me wish that I could be transported over the sea to those wonderful places where truth and justice reigned and good always triumphed over evil.

Action adventures about a Caribbean that never existed made me dream of those glory days when it was easier to distinguish good guys from bad ones and where the hero and heroine lived happily ever. These books and movies were works of fiction, but they filled my head with dreams and I swore that someday I would see for myself those lands where swashbuckling pirates once flew the Jolly Roger. It was a dumb reason to leave home, but to this day I still can't think of a better reason to see the world, or at least part of it.

But I was nagged by two questions when I returned stateside. Why were we so rich when the people in the islands were so poor? And, why were so many locals still laboring with their bodies for low pay when we back home were quickly pursuing white collar careers? It took me years to appreciate the economic retardation caused by centuries of colonial rule and prevailing mercantilist theories.

A- Few people spread over many islands

I had no idea how many people called Nassau home; nor did I know how many people lived in the Bahamas. I did eventually extrapolate data from the 1975 West Indies and Caribbean Yearbook that the archipelago's population in the mid 1950's was slightly less than 125,000. [1]

I did the same computations for the entire region and concluded that the West Indies had a population of about 20 million, including the West Indian states that hugged the Caribbean coasts of Central and South America. This was a vast expanse of land and sea occupied by relatively few people.

The region's population has grown over the years, and today it stands at about 35 million, according to the latest World Bank data. [2] Growth has been fairly evenly distributed except in the English speaking East Caribbean states, the focus of this book, where it has been lower. The average longevity of people has also improved, rising from about 55 to 60 years of age to the 75 -78 range (the same as it is for high income countries) except for Haiti where the average lifespan is lower. One startling difference in demographic patterns between the present and the 1950's in the English speaking eastern Caribbean are the current waves of emigration by local nationals to North America and Europe and the counter flood of immigration from Central and South America.

B- Why write about the English speaking East Caribbean?

England's former colonies in the eastern Caribbean are unique in the sense that they have all evolved as constitutional democracies with a mix of open market capitalism and socialist government oversight to protect their people from runaway private enterprise. These are not inconsequential feats when their small size and limited influence in a world of mega-power politics are taken into consideration. These new states are among the smallest and most vulnerable in the world, and yet they have succeeded in surviving and even in growing their economies. They have also been able to hold their own in the world power structure and to impact the foreign political and economic policies of their much better heeled trading and investment partners.

The problem is that in the thirty to forty years since their independence they have not yet closed the income gap that exists between them and their wealthy neighbors. Why this situation has come to exist, how it is being addressed, and what the prognosis is for closing the income inequality gap are the subjects analyzed in this book. This book contends that the existing income inequality in the islands is due to the unequal footing created in the colonial era and perpetuated by their current economic policies and relations with their major trading and investment partners.

C- Ethnicity, Race and Religion

The impact of demographic change on environments did not register with me as a teenager. It simply dawned on me that there were many different looking poor people co-existing in small crowded towns and villages apart from a few grand homes and estates. There were many different races but Black and its different shades were dominant colors. There were also many different churches. In the English and Dutch speaking states, Protestantism and its major denominations predominated while Catholicism was the rule in the French and Spanish speaking islands.

D- Climate and Topography

The Caribbean was supposed to be bright and sunny, but I saw much rain and little sun in the ramshackle villages and one room huts that clawed the shore and the steep rugged hills where families lived with no running water, no electricity, no inside bathroom and in which meals were cooked over an open fire or on a stove using wood or anything else that burned. And then there was the smell that never went away; it was more of a stench than a smell, and I began to notice that chronic poverty had a foul odor, the kind that fills the air when people can't get themselves clean and enjoy a sanitary environment and where food spoils quickly when there is no refrigeration. It was not so bad near the beach, but it was worse inland and away from ready sources of water. And the water; it was scarce and foul tasting and needed to be boiled.

E- Poverty and Wealth

Soap was a luxury not heaped upon the poor. I found the squalid, grinding poverty quaint and even attractive at first. After all, it was like living close to nature. It was only many years later that I realized that my accepting attitude was based on the fact that I was not doomed to live that way forever. I knew that someday I would return home to a life of relative comfort and prosperity in a world filled with all the conveniences of modern technology.

If the poor were very poor, the rich were very rich. The problem was that most of the people were depressingly poor and very few were rich. I noticed something else; most of the poor were non-White, and most of the rich were White. I did meet wealthy non-Whites who held high positions in the White dominated governments, but they were few in number. I was too young at the time to understand that especially in the English West Indies political independence was looming on the horizon and that the colonial overlords were in fact grooming politically active locals for eventual self-government.

I worked for a while on an old island steamer. Life was good and there was always plenty of food. We plowed our way across the Bahamas, Turks and Caicos, past Haiti and the Dominican Republic and on to Puerto Rico where we stopped in San Juan to refuel before sailing on to Viequez, Culebra, the US Virgin Islands and the UK Virgin Islands. From there we chugged on to the Leeward and Windward Islands that made up the Lesser Antilles. Most of our stops were in the English speaking islands.

F- No place for a tan

I have a confession to make. I worshipped the bronze tan on people when I was young, and that was one of the reasons that drove me to the Caribbean.

That was a judgment error. I arrived at the start of the hurricane season, and even without the hurricanes it was the rainy season and there were numerous storms of varying intensity and violence that wrought havoc throughout the islands. More than half of the time, our vessel was out of action, holed up in some tropical hurricane hole without cool air and water to wait out a storm.

Small storms were short and cut a narrow swath of destruction but major hurricane systems took a longer time to work their way through the islands and ended up leveling entire communities that took years to recover. This sort of bad weather was not an incident of a single year. It was part of the Caribbean geography and Caribbean hurricanes have been chronicled over the centuries by European explorers, and they are an annual phenomenon today. The problem with hurricanes in the islands is that their destruction created takes years to repair. More recent storms have not only wiped out material progress but have set back many local economies for years to come.

G- Earthquakes and Volcanoes

Someone told me when I was in St. Lucia that the Caribbean had many volcanoes and was prone to earth tremors and occasional volcanic eruptions. St. Lucia had a dead volcano; Grenada had an offshore underwater volcano and Montserrat had a volcano, but it had never erupted in recorded history. That same person said the Caribbean basin was an unstable, jellified bowl of volcanic activity. How interesting, and I went off to have a beer.

Martinique had a volcano called Mont Pelee. It blew its top in 1902 and is said to have caused widespread devastation, killing 30,000 people within a couple of minutes. [3]

Montserrat's Soufriere volcano awoke in the mid-nineties and made half of the island uninhabitable. [4]

And so, I know better today. Volcanic action and tremors are part of the region's geology and history and are undoubtedly factored into all the risk assessments made by businesses considering long term investments in some of the islands. Guarantees safeguarding such investments from acts of nature are limited and reduce the pace of economic activity.

II- The Good Old Days

It is this group of islands plus the US and UK Virgin Islands and Barbados that is addressed in this book on the English Speaking Eastern Caribbean. I call them "islands in the wind" because they face the trade winds that sweep in from West Africa. These states, many of them sovereign nations today, are constantly buffeted not only by the trade winds that bring hurricanes in their wake, but by the fiercer winds of global economic, social and political change.

This is not to suggest that times were better during the long colonial era that lasted four and a half centuries into the mid 1900's from the very late 1400,'s, but I had a healthy teenager's ignorance of history and failed to understand that storybook and cinematic depictions of the Caribbean were misleading. The so-called "good old days" were largely fictional, and the colonial overlords in the eastern Caribbean were cruel and barbaric to a fault. The prevailing political systems were autocratic to make sure that the colonies existed to serve the interests of their European conquerors. Total control over human life was the order of the days, creating an oppressive environment made worse by the legalization of slavery. When slavery was finally abolished in the English speaking Caribbean colonies in 1834, it was estimated that over 90% of their populations were slaves of African origin,

A- From Slavery to Freedom

The long lonely struggle for political independence started in 1834 with the emancipation of the slaves and reached its climax in the 1950's. I cannot boast about having been part of that critical transition period in the islands; I was there, but I was also blind to what was going on. Little things however did not escape my notice although they held little meaning for me. Customs inspectors at the docks at the various ports of entry for example were mostly non-White locals. Uniformed police were also non-White as were the many minor bureaucrats, teachers, office workers and store employees who I met during my travels. Political change was in process, and within twenty years of my first trip to the islands, total independence or internal self-governing status was a fact if life.

III- Political Realities

Some independence movements are short, contentious and bloody. In the English speaking Caribbean, and especially in the Lesser Antilles, they were drawn out but relatively peaceful. I for one did not feel the change. I might be accused of cultural blindness; however, I happened to be in Cuba a few years later when Fidel Castro and his followers made their final push and marched into Havana. That was change, and when his army entered the city, there was an exodus of people to leave the country the following day. My recollection was that flights and ferries were jammed with tourists and the minions of the once thriving tourist industry making a beeline for Key West and Miami.

The change in the English speaking Caribbean was more subtle. The local governmental structure was not being altered. It was only the administration of power that was changing hands. Free and open elections were already a fact of life, and in short order many chief ministers would become prime ministers or presidents as their states attained full independence and full national sovereignty. Already, the political heads of these emerging nations and states were meeting to discuss the creation of a regional trade bloc that was to become by 1958 the West Indies Federation, an organization that was to morph into the Caribbean Free Trade Association in 1964 and morph once again into the Caribbean Common Market in 1973, a consortium of trading nations that continues to thrive today.

A- The political emancipation of the majority

Other races and ethnic groups were represented in the demographic mix as well, Chinese, East Indian, Arab, etc, and they all seemed to be doing better than the Blacks in 1954. However, what I failed to see was that the existing power structure was already endorsing the rights of the local population to self-government and to the selection of their own leaders. It would be just a matter of time before the Black racial majority would have a firm handle on the reigns of government.

Vere Cornwall Bird of Antigua, Grantley Adams of Barbados, Eric Gairy of Grenada, Alexander Bustamante and Norman Manley of Jamaica and Eric Williams of Trinidad and Tobago were rapidly becoming household names, and by the end of the 1950s' independence was approaching reality and the political dog fights in the islands featured Black on Black competition. And the buzz was all about some guy named Fidel Castro who was trying to take over Cuba. It was clear that the islands' political and economic landscape was about to change forever.

The old colonial arrangements were comfortable in a way. They made it easier for everyone to deal with the subtle and not so subtle nuances of the existing economic, political and social pecking order. Future prospects were intimidating. I knew nothing at the time about constitutional democracy or dictatorship and "isms" like totalitarianism, socialism and communism. I had crude ideas but had no clear educated convictions. Years later I learned that my fear of change was shared by others who dedicated their professional lives studying and helping to shape the region's future. Would change be violent or peaceful? Would the new democracies last or would they turn to dictatorship? Would they accept capitalism as economic doctrine or would they adopt socialist or even communist ideas to address issues of economic growth and development? These questions linger to this day.

2

So Poor And Democratic

I- The problem with bananas

I could not help observing during my trip that all sorts of manufactured goods were being shipped to the islands and that ships were returning to the States with an assortment of commodities and cottage industry products like baskets, hand carved wooden statues and rum. I attributed this exchange to the nature of trade with the islands. It was eighteenth century mercantilism *a la* Adam Smith's theory of absolute advantage at its best. It was also a great formula for economic stagnation and retardation.

The former English colonies were evolving into constitutional democracies but their economies were in a time warp and in no way prepared to compete successfully in global markets. They were feudal, "latafundia" economies in which power and wealth was determined by one's landholdings from which commodities could be extracted and exported. All that was needed to make the system work were cheap labor, seed capital and foreign connections, So, from their colonial beginnings, the emerging states were export oriented and dependent upon the more developed countries of the world. They were in a world in which commodity prices were set not in the Caribbean but on Wall Street. Therefore, while it is a fact that for the most part, many races and religions have learned to live in relative harmony on society's lower rungs, the power, influence and wealth of the islands are concentrated in the hands of a few families (no color line here) who control the factors of production, have access to financial markets and have global connections.

Economic opportunities and the potential for upward mobility have been limited by this concentration of wealth and income and have led to outbound migration, a phenomenon I encountered in 1954. I was about to return to the States and had been befriended by a Grenadian customs official who wanted very badly to leave. I asked him why, and he replied, "The worst that you have in America is far better than the best that we have in Grenada."

A- Cheap rum, bad gin and no ice

And so those picture postcard villages bordered by palm trees inching up the hillside from the baby blue waters of the Caribbean, where pirates and buccaneers once presumably played, were nothing more than impoverished economic backwaters whose destinies were not their own. Not only were the people poor, they were basically destitute, huddled in makeshift shanties and scraping together a meager subsistence existence from fishing, farming and laboring on the few commercial plantations that were left. There was plenty of rum, but the gin was bad, water needed to be boiled and ice was a thing of luxury. Luckier people worked for the government, happily beholden to the favors of the wealthy families and bureaucracies that ran their society.

What struck me was how inexpensive rum was even at full retail per shot in bars. Of course, rum was the beverage of choice (beer cost more) for the poor. It came from sugar and sugar cane was everywhere. It provided food and drink in one thin stalk and it grew like a weed. Gin was a favorite with the rich, the near rich and would-be rich. It was slightly more expensive, but the local brands were not too good. Still, drinking was cheaper than eating.

The problem, I found out, was more than booze and good food; it was the water and the lack of a readily available source of energy to generate power. Water came from wells. It was scarce and not very potable, having always to be boiled or otherwise heavily treated. Ice boats could still be seen making the rounds in the middle of the last century, especially in Spring time, but ice had a short shelf life in the tropics without refrigeration, a novel technology in the Caribbean.

Industrial refrigeration was an innovation being introduced from the United States into larger markets like Puerto Rico and had not yet spread to the smaller islands. Even electricity was a rarity. True, the boat I worked on carried a few used refrigerators and even a couple of new ones, but they were destined for use by a few wealthy families who had their own generators and energy sources. Local hotels, stores and offices had electric lighting, but candles for emergencies were daily necessities.

Time and technology have largely solved energy issues from a supply side perspective (cost remains high) and candles have largely disappeared from hotels, but water shortages are chronic and widespread and probably attest to the limits of population growth and of economic growth and development in the eastern Caribbean. Desalination plants are a solution and have been built on many islands, but their operating costs are exorbitant.

I saw a pecking order with the domesticated animals at the bottom and the great landowners and business entrepreneurs at the top. In the small villages, chickens squawked and pigs squealed and bleating goats ran free on unpaved streets, and the few cows and oxen roaming about had seen better times. But they were so important to survival that under local law, absconding with any one of those poor creatures was often considered a crime.

The poorest people were Black, meaning that they originally came from Africa as slaves between the mid 1500's and early 1800's. The pirate tales I read never talked about them, but I learned much later that after almost three centuries of slave importation Blacks now amounted to a great majority of the region's population. Unless Blacks wrung their way into government and politics, as many eventually did with varying degrees of success, they lived pretty much near the bottom of the socioeconomic order, faring hardly better than their farm animals.

B- The Economic Dilemma

The fundamental problem then, and it remains a basic issue today, is that bananas, sugar, coffee and tobacco are no longer reasons for nations to wage war. The lack of global demand for such commodity type output has limited the region's economic and political clout in the international arena. Attempts to change the economic configuration of the islands by shifting from labor intensive agriculture and cottage industries to more capital and technology intensive enterprises like tourism and financial services have met with some success, but they are still works in progress whose scorecard is incomplete.

II- Flexing international muscles

The region's colonial status prevented it from participating in international organizations; its interests were represented by its overseas overlords. That changed as individual states became independent and began taking seats in the United Nations, the World Bank and the International Monetary Fund.

Independence also brought them representation and voting rights in regional groups like the Organization of American States, the Caribbean Common Market and Community and, for the former English colonies in the eastern Caribbean, the Association of East Caribbean States. This has allowed the small eastern Caribbean states to band together to collectively promote their own special interests.

III- Challenges and Opportunities

In retrospect, I think it was that fear of change that finally convinced me to return to the States and resume my studies. But most of my concerns were groundless, especially in the new English speaking states. The previous half century of England's tutelage gave birth to constitutional democracies on the English model that embraced a moderate center-left philosophy of economic action still in vogue today.

Temporary setbacks under the tenure of Antigua's Bird family, and under the short lived rule of Maurice Bishop in Grenada notwithstanding, the area has enjoyed an almost fifty year period of peace and stability. I was far too young to appreciate the nuances of these changes in the islands the first time I visited, but I did see other problems, aside from the nagging poverty, much of which still exists in stubborn pockets throughout the region.

One was the lack of opportunity, and it was that which probably convinced me that my future in the islands was limited. I thought of sticking it out and using the advantage of color and class to promote my needs (in retrospect, an almost fatal error of hubris and conceit), but I decided that I was better off going home, finishing school and looking for a job in a much larger and more diverse labor marketplace.

If we move that decision a half century forward to the present, my return to the States was probably well advised. Good, high paying job opportunities were truly limited in the islands. Indeed, it is noteworthy that emigration by people in the eastern Caribbean has been and continues to impact its growth and development. To date, the so-called brain drain goes on unabated. There are, for example, more Grenadians living in Canada, the United States and England than in Grenada.

A- Plenty of bananas, sugar and spice and sunshine

"The living is easy here," a friend once told me. "You can live off the land, we have plenty of bananas, sugar cane, and we have limes, lemons and other fruits and veggies and fish."

And so if I wanted to enjoy a subsistence existence, the islands could be my home. Or, I could become a multi-acre landowner and grow these basic commodities for export. It never dawned on me until later that the region's permanent economic problem was staring me down. The global market for basic plantation type commodities like bananas was soft when I visited the islands the first time, and it remains soft today, if the pun may be allowed.

What was more disturbing was the total lack of differentiation among the islands. Each island had its own personality and unique features, but they also had too much in common. Sugar, bananas, cottage industry goods and warm weather in winter were common denominators rendering them hostage to price setters in their industrialized trading partners. Barbados had sugar, and from the sugar came rum. Saint Lucia had bananas; Grenada had spices; and Saint Kitts and Nevis grew limes. In a purely macroeconomic context, whoever supplied the refrigerators and the air conditioning equipment could decide how many bananas it could demand in exchange. It was the classical mercantilist model that England once tried to impose on its North American colonies. Great Britain would ship manufactured goods in exchange for raw materials.

And that was the real economic problem facing the islands I visited. They were specializing in labor-intensive and low value added products, selling them abroad for capital-intensive, high value-added manufactured goods. It was not a good deal for the islands and it did not take a long time for me to realize that it gave them very unfavorable terms of trade. It was a scenario in which the region could be impoverished by enjoying a merchandise trade surplus coupled to unfavorable trade terms.

IV- Education, work and the drift of life

I returned from the islands at the end of that memorable summer feeling a bit dejected. It was a mere adolescent adventure, adults explained upon my return, and they advised me to finish my education and get a job. And so by chance I took some courses with Thomas Adam, a professor of political science and constitutional law. His lectures opened my mind to the great complexity of civilized society and made it possible for me later in life to fit the experiences of my journey into the broader context of a career that could dovetail with my growing interest in development economics. Much of what I saw as tropical islands basking in the cooling trade winds understated their importance and potential in the world and the commonalities they shared with many other emerging markets elsewhere in the world. It took me years to understand that these brand new Caribbean states had the same problems of all societies, namely, how to build democratic institutions on the political side, and how to improve living standards on the economic side.

Thomas A. Adam was a firm believer in the English constitutional system of law and government and also believed that societies could not grow their economies unless they embraced the principle of open markets. He was also well traveled, interested as he was in the evolution of England's remaining overseas possessions from dependency to independence. And in the late 1950's, when I was in college, many of England's former colonies in the world were either fully independent (India and Pakistan) or on the way to independence with parliamentary systems (Barbados and Grenada).

However, the book he authored was a comparative political systems work titled, "Government and Politics in Africa South of the Sahara," published by Random house in 1959. I had not visited Africa but the book shaped my opinions of how emerging states might set the stepping stones from colonial dependency to competitive independence. Very unfortunately, the dream of constitutional democracy has eluded many African countries, and that must have aggravated professor Adam as the years wore on. He should have perhaps traveled to the West Indies instead. [1]

Another book that shaped my ideas was a work recommended by Thomas Adam that was authored by Justin S. Furnivall called "Colonial Policy and Practice, A Comparative Study of Burma and Netherlands India." [2] It was a great read, but both Burma (now Myanmar) and Indonesia (then the Dutch East Indies) transitioned into dictatorships with limited open markets. While

Indonesia has been building democratic institutions and promoting a market oriented economy, Myanmar is still bound to its military oligarchs. In any case, these books, now safely locked away in my small library of historical references, served as object lessons about the frailty of constitutional forms of government when societies are faced with the tasks of national survival in a hostile environment.

V- A Personal Unplanned Journey to the Eastern Caribbean

The basic personal problem I had was that I never had a plan and this was the easiest and fastest way to jump-start making a living. After finishing my schooling and a stint in the Army, I worked for Societe Rhone Poulenc's (Sanoflis Aventis today) New York office as export manager until I was fired. My next job was as export sales manager for the Mennen Company (today part of Colgate Palmolive).

I soon forgot about Africa and Asia in favor of the Caribbean and Latin America where Mennen had its bread and butter export markets. And when I left Mennen to teach college and start an import-export sales business, it was natural that I would concentrate on the English speaking West Indies where I was already well connected. It did not take long for the Caribbean's eastern fringe of new states to become my principal market. The shortest distance between poverty and prosperity is a straight line, and for me that line ran directly from New Jersey to the West Indies.

In time, I began thinking back to Tom Adam and Justin Furnivall who had such hope for their countries of interest. It was increasingly obvious that the goals of democracy and economic prosperity in many African countries, in Burma and in many other countries were not being met. Indeed, it took me years to realize that freedom and independence from whatever a rebelling society thought held it in bounds did not necessarily mean that democracy was the automatic default choice. Many countries turned to the autocratic despotism of a totalitarian dictatorship with varying degrees of success and failure in their attempts to craft growth oriented economic systems.

VI- Purpose of the book

This is why I felt the English speaking eastern Caribbean states deserved a closer look in terms of their economic and political evolution. It would have been easy to conclude that the new states, perhaps because of their poverty and limited self-governing experience, would drift into dictatorship. After all, that was the experience of the Dominican Republic, Haiti and many of the countries of Central and South America.

I was consequently happy to see that in fact the former English colonies in the eastern Caribbean were able to maintain their democratic institutions. I was somewhat distressed by the region's lagging economies and therefore decided to devote this book to the analysis of the political economies of the English speaking East Caribbean to see how the region has fared to date, how its individual states have made the transformation from poor and middle income societies, and what they must do to become high income globally competitive nations.

A- Format and organization of the book

The title for this book, "Islands in the Wind," was picked because of the geographic location of the English speaking east Caribbean states. They are in the Leeward and Windward Islands, a convex arc of islands cooled by the trade winds blowing across the Atlantic from northwestern Africa over the North Equatorial Current. The Leeward group begins with the UK and US Virgin Islands east of Puerto Rico and runs southeast to Anguilla, Antigua and Barbuda, Montserrat, Saint Kitts and Nevis and Dominica. The states in the Windward group are Saint Lucia, Saint Vincent and the Grenadines and Grenada. Barbados is also included with the Windward group in this book despite the fact that it is located a hundred miles east of the arc in the middle of the Atlantic Ocean.

The format of this book is to examine the background, historical, political, economic and international environments impacting the development of the individual states. I have also done a SWOT analysis (Strengths, Weaknesses, Opportunities and Threats) to recommend future courses of action that might be considered to accelerate the processes of economic growth.

As a convenience to readers, I have placed all references under "Notes" and under "Acknowledgements, Attributions and Credits" at the end of the book. Much of the information and data has been derived from commonly accessible Internet sources and can be easily accessed for updates.

3

The English Speaking East Caribbean

I- The keys to independent survival

I have often wondered how the tiny former English colonies in the East Caribbean have managed to survive as sovereign states in the years since achieving independence. The answer to the question lies in Mohamed Ali's (Cassius Marcellus Clay Jr.) formula for winning in the boxing ring: "Float like a butterfly, sting like a bee. Your eyes can't hit what your eyes can't see." [1]

This is the marvel of these Caribbean states. Their economies have grown without drawing undue attention from richer and more powerful nations. But neither democracy nor dictatorship can guarantee ongoing economic growth and development which depends on a stock of savings that can be tapped to support an open investment faucet. And yet, resource poor and perpetually under financed, they have succeeded in building constitutional democracies that hold court over societies using a mix capitalist and socialist economic principles with varying degrees of success. The purpose of this book is to show how the small English speaking islands in the Eastern Caribbean have coped with constraints that have destabilized larger states in the region. [2]

Eleven states, ten former English colonies and one American possession, are included in this study. The UK and US Virgin Islands are possessions and therefore do not have a prime minister and legal status as full fledged sovereign nation states. Two states (Anguilla and

Montserrat) allow their foreign policy to be shaped by England and are therefore governed by a Chief Minister who has no diplomatic portfolio. Interestingly, Anguilla is an associate member of the Organization of Eastern Caribbean States (OECS) while Montserrat is a full member. The UK Virgins (BVI's, as they are more commonly called) maintain an associate relationship with the OECS.

The other seven states (Antigua, Barbados, Dominica, Grenada, Saint Kitts and Nevis, Saint Lucia, Saint Vincent and the Grenadines) all have national sovereignty and are governed by a Prime Minister as the head of government with full diplomatic powers. They are voting members of the OECS (except for Barbados which maintains associate member status). They also belong to the United Nations, the World Bank, the World Trade Organization, the International Monetary Fund, the World Health Organization and other international organizations. If these east Caribbean states are included in the greater West Indies, many of them English speaking as well, they can form a 25 country voting bloc out of 192 countries in the U.N., better than 12% of the membership in the world body. [3] This can be a major foreign policy factor for the US to consider as Venezuela, with Russian assistance, seeks to expand its influence throughout the Caribbean. [4]

The English speaking eastern Caribbean states have a total population that is less than 900,000, [5], spread over lush tropical islands, most comparable in size to holiday destinations like Martha's Vineyard, Nantucket Island and Catalina Island. [6] Except for the weather and agricultural commodities like sugar and bananas they have no high demand natural resources such as oil to bring them great income and wealth. The average annual per capita Gross Domestic Product for each state ranges from US$ 8,000 to US$20,000, less than the average American annual per capita GDP of over $40,000. [7]

But size belies importance and small size cannot be dismissed out of hand, and this is where the national security perspective comes into play. These island nations were important enough for England and the United States to intervene in their internal affairs on several occasions in the past decades, and the U.S. today continues to be actively engaged in the region.

The United Kingdom was instrumental in paving the way for the islands' independence, an effort that extends back to the early part of the twentieth century. But when sovereignty finally arrived the U.K. still had to send troops to Anguilla in 1967 to keep the peace. [8] And the U.S., less than twenty years later, invaded and temporarily seized the reigns of power in Grenada. [9]. Washington also spent many sleepless nights agonizing over the antics of the Bird family dynasty in Antigua that ultimately affected the state's political stability.

The United States has now replaced the United Kingdom as the patron and financial-economic benefactor of the English speaking east Caribbean states despite the fact that it is not one of its major trading partners. This speaks all too loudly to the importance of the region to American interests. The country can little afford to be confronted with an array of potentially hostile states on its southeastern flank. The strategic importance of the Caribbean's eastern rim from a military standpoint has diminished as the technology of warfare has reduced the need for the physical presence of bases and troops. Neither are the region's economies all that important to the American mainland. But these island states, all having very sizeable émigré population in permanent residence in the United States, can create a security issue if their sentiments and loyalties shift away from North America to embrace the populism and authoritarianism of countries like Venezuela and its allies.

II- The English speaking East Caribbean states

The countries under study in this book are, in alphabetical order: Anguilla, Antigua, Barbados, Dominica, Grenada, Montserrat, Saint Kitts and Nevis, Saint Lucia, Saint Vincent and the Grenadines, The US Virgin Islands and UK Virgin Islands. All of these states are full OECS members except for the US, UK Virgin Islands and Barbados (which has expressed interest but has not yet joined). Anguilla and the British Virgin Islands are British overseas territories by choice and are associate members. Montserrat is a special case. It is a British overseas territory but a full OECS member. This odd situation seems to have resulted from the Soufriere Hills volcano eruption that struck the island in the 1995 and destroyed Plymouth, the capital city. [10]

A- How the system works

The political system of the region shares many commonalities with that of the United Kingdom which subscribes to a parliamentary government under a limited monarchy. This means that the head of state is the monarch and the head of government is a prime minister selected by the political party that has won a majority vote in a general election. Prime ministers representing a coalition of minority parties when no majority exists are also possible. The prime minister governs with the assistance of a cabinet whose members are chosen from all key political parties, including the major minority parties, thereby creating a built-in "loyal opposition." The prime minister's powers are shared with an elected parliament (legislature) and with an independent judiciary. This is the system that evolved over the centuries in England and it has largely been mirrored by its former Caribbean colonies.

Fully independent states in the region (Barbados, Dominica and Grenada as examples) are governed by a prime minister. Fully self-governing states

(Anguilla for example) are governed by a chief minister. In all cases, power is shared with either a two-party or multi-party cabinet and legislature with the participation of an independent judiciary. In all states, a constitutional guarantee is made to preserve the representation and power of the so-called "loyal opposition." Hence, the minority parties (the larger ones at least) are guaranteed a say and a vote in the deliberations and decisions of the cabinet and parliament.

The interests of the "Crown," (London) is represented by a royal emissary (a royal governor) appointed by the reigning monarch (Queen Elizabeth II). The local government in power generally gives its express or tacit approval to these appointments. The tendency in recent years has been for London to choose a local national for the post. The position is largely ceremonial; but it assumes importance when issues emerge involving collective action through the Commonwealth of Nations to which England and all its former colonies are members.

Those states with a prime minister of course field foreign embassies and can host permanent foreign legations. Those with chief ministers have their foreign interests represented by England and its overseas embassies and thus cannot have diplomatic relations with other countries.

This political system is the English speaking eastern Caribbean's strongest suite and goes a long way to preserving its political stability. What is even more amazing is that it took root and evolved in societies that were largely slave-based with little or no experience in self-government. Indeed, the very processes of political emancipation leading to self-government did not really begin until the 1950's, although slavery as a legal institution had been absent by then for more than a century. In addition, the local inhabitants often had to combat a general feeling among their White neighbors and often reluctant mentors that Blacks (who as descendants of slaves were the majority of the population) were not intellectually equipped to govern themselves let alone manage their destinies as independent states. [11]

The historical fact is that by the 1950's the pace of independence gathered momentum so that within a generation, all the former English colonies in the region had achieved self-governing status including the US Virgin Islands.

B-The problem of externalities

The real problems that faced the former colonies and which bedevils them to this day are the externalities of weather and geology. The east Caribbean region is volcanic and poses a constant threat to its economic growth and to its development. The weather is an even more serious matter. It is warm all year around but is prone to hurricanes and violent storms that leave a wide path of destruction in their wake. This inclement weather is the big recurring threat faced by the islands and is a source of great expense. There have been many instances when progress slowly and painfully made was wiped out in minutes with much loss of life and property. Adding to the bad weather and unfortunate geology is the knowledge that the region's economic fortunes are too closely linked to those of the more developed nations of the world. An economic downturn in the United States, Europe and elsewhere can too often lead to prolonged economic misfortune at home.

These are the major challenges facing the people of the English speaking eastern Caribbean. How these challenges are managed will be addressed in this book when the individual countries are analyzed.

C- The OECS [12]

This section would be incomplete without considering the role played by the Organization of Eastern Caribbean States (OECS) in building a climate of political and economic cooperation among the English speaking eastern Caribbean states. The OECS came into existence in 1981 for purposes of encouraging good governance in accordance to principles of constitutional democracy. Its role was also to promote economic growth and development through international cooperation leading to the allocation of resources for hurricane and other disaster recovery programs.

It was a creation of the Treaty of Basseterre, the capital city of Saint Kitts and Nevis, replacing the West Indies Associated States (WISA), an informal organization formed in 1967 as the entire English speaking West Indies was moving rapidly towards self-governing status and/ or independence. WISA, as the parent prototype for OECS, failed because its member states, still in the shadow of colonialism, had not fully crystallized their political identities in terms of how they wanted to be organized and function as nation states. Separatist movements sprouted up in Barbuda, Anguilla and Nevis. The Barbuda effort failed but Anguilla succeeded in breaking away from its union with St. Kitts and Nevis to remain a British Overseas Territory. [13]

In the years following 1967, full independence came to WISA members in quick order. Grenada was first in 1974 followed by Dominica in 1978, Saint Lucia and Saint Vincent in 1979, Antigua and Barbuda in 1981 and Saint Kitts and Nevis in 1983.

The OECS succeeded where WISA failed as the former English colonies in the Leeward and Windward Islands, now comfortable in their new skins, realized that some sort of international association was needed to address issues that could not be managed in a cost-effective manner individually by the tiny nations. The OECS, with its Secretariat in Castries, Saint Lucia, is the association's executive and representative institution. Its four sections, Corporate Services, Economic Affairs, Functional Cooperation and External Relations, are charged with the responsibility of developing policies that can be embraced by the member countries with their consent. It also advances the interests of its members through its offices in Belgium (the European Union), Canada and the United States.

The Eastern Caribbean Supreme Court (ECSC) is part of the OECS and serves as the court of appeals on judicial cases coming up from the member states. From the ECSC, cases can be further appealed to the Caribbean Court of Justice (CCJ) located in Port-of-Spain, Trinidad and Tobago. The CCJ is relatively new (2003). Until it began its operation, appeals from the ECSC went directly to the Privy Council in London. There is to date no universal acceptance of the CCJ's jurisdiction among the OECS members.

The OECS has its own central bank, the Eastern Caribbean Central Bank (ECCB). It is the group's monetary authority and has oversight authority over the monetary policies of its members. Its main responsibility in this connection is to support the region's currency, the East Caribbean Dollar (XCD), which is pegged to the U.S. Dollar at about 2.7 XCD per U.S. Dollar.

Two successes can be credited to the OECS. One is hurricane relief, and the other has been in upholding the value of the pegged foreign exchange rate. The OECS has been responsible for coordinating the financing and logistics of hurricane and storm relief and recovery operations since the 1980's. An equally daunting but more invisible challenge has been to keep the currency stable in the face of regional trade deficits that have not always been offset by private investment inflows. To this end, the OECS has built close relationships with the World Bank, other development banks and with the United States to ensure financial assistance when necessary.

Another sign of OECS success is its growing appeal to other non-affiliated island states in the surrounding Caribbean area. The British Virgin Islands has requested to be considered for full membership. That request has been positively received by the OECS and is currently awaiting a decision from England. Transition from colonial dependency to independence under the umbrella of the OECS would need to include a switch from Pound Sterling to the East Caribbean Dollar as the reigning currency, essentially moving residents all BVI residents into a weaker currency by virtue of the XCD peg to the US Dollar. This might raise merchandise import costs in general but lower costs for American tourists, an important tradeoff argument for and against union with the OECS that remains to be resolved.

A similar situation exists with the U.S. Virgin Islands. It too has expressed interest in becoming part of the OECS. Aside from the fact that this would ultimately involve total political separation from the United States, a matter that Washington might wish to avoid for national security reasons, a new set of relationships would emerge that may not be always to the advantage of the U.S. Virgins. Because of the peg, a currency switch from the US$ to the XCD would be the least of the challenges faced. There would need to be, for starters, a total revamping of the legal and judicial systems that presently fit within the standards and practices of American law and jurisprudence. The much deeper issue that will need to be addressed is that of national identity from a cultural perspective. U.S. Virgin Islanders will need to have to decide whether they "feel" American or "West Indian." That may end up being such a divisive issue that it might not be worth while exploring anytime soon.

The OECS does not function in a vacuum in the Caribbean and is itself associated with larger organizations in the region. It is represented in the Caribbean Community and Common Market (CARICOM), the successor to the older Caribbean Free Trade Association that was started in 1965 after the dissolution of the even older West Indies Federation that was formed in 1958. Indeed, all OECS members belong to CARICOM as self-governing states in their own right.

The OECS states, along with Barbados and every other Caribbean nation, also belong to the Organization of American States (OAS) that includes all the countries of Latin America and the Caribbean. The OAS was a creation of American foreign policy in the 1930's and still serves as a forum for the discussion and resolution of issues of common interest. It also serves as a bully pulpit for the United States, its biggest and most powerful member.

The OECS and its members in turn must remain sensitive to ever shifting U.S. sentiments, forcing them to often walk a diplomatic tightrope between their interests and those of their powerful neighbors. Still, working in unison through the OECS gives each country more power to influence events than by working alone.

Finally, they are economic and financial beneficiaries of the International Monetary Fund (IMF), the World Bank, the Caribbean Development Bank (CDB), the U.S. Export-Import Bank (EXIM

Bank), the Caribbean Basin Initiative (CBI), the U.S. Agency for International Development (USAID), the Overseas Private Investment Corporation (OPIC) and the U.S. Peace Corp. These organizations are heavily funded by the United States and provide much of the region's financing and assistance for its growth and development. These institutions are giants in their own right and can easily overwhelm their tiny clients with their often ponderous rules and regulations. This is where the old and overused cliché that "a house divided cannot stand," works to the advantage of the OECS and its member states.

D- Five Points of American interest

The United States has always had an overriding interest in Caribbean affairs, and that includes the eastern Caribbean region. It is for that reason that it keeps a constant vigil in the region through a discreet but strong diplomatic and military presence. Washington has close diplomatic ties with the OECS and its individual associated states. These are further strengthened by membership in the Organization of American States (OAS) that embraces all nations in the Western Hemisphere. As the Caribbean's sole military custodian, a role that the United States assumed after the Spanish-American War of 1898, American air and naval forces unobtrusively patrol the region's waters and airspace. This watchful eye reflects five points of national interest.

1- The tourism factor

More than one million Americans visit the islands each year as cruise ship day trippers or as vacationers who do at least one overnight or more in one or several of the islands. Many thousands more now come from Canada, Europe, Asia and Africa on their own or as part of organized tour groups. This requires a security cordon that only the U.S. can afford to mount. Why it allocates tax payer revenues to this effort probably stems from the fact that tourism has become central to the area's economic growth and development, playing a more important role than the traditional agricultural sector of sugar and bananas. Policing the area with American air and naval power, largely unseen by all concerned, has been and continues to be a form of "invisible" economic assistance.

2- The National Security factor

The region is the easternmost part of a much larger Caribbean circling the southeastern flank of the United States. If that circle is expanded to cover the entire West Indies, then Bermuda, the Bahamas, Belize, French Guiana, Guyana and Suriname would also be included. Washington has always considered this extended perimeter as critical to its national security and therefore within its sphere of influence. Its simple dogma is that the presence of states with hostile ideologies and policies cannot be accepted and states that cannot govern themselves cannot be tolerated. This explains why it has intervened in Caribbean affairs so often and why it goes to great lengths to support the area's economy. It cannot afford to see an unfriendly political situation arise on its flanks.

3- American foreign policy objectives

This concerns the political and economic relations between the English speaking east Caribbean countries and the United States. It is probably true that if the region was to disappear from the face of the Earth, its passing would be mostly unnoticed by its North American neighbors, except that perhaps the price of sugar and bananas might go up and more tourists would flock to Florida. However, the U.S. has long held as a cornerstone of foreign policy that countries with democratic institutions and capitalist practices made for the best long term allies in the arena of international power politics.

While this thesis might not always hold true on close examination, it has nevertheless shaped U.S. policy in the eastern Caribbean. Assistance to bolster local economies has long flowed in through a variety of policy programs like the Caribbean Basin Initiative (CBI) and United States Aid for International Development (USAID). Financial support has also come through the various international organizations wholly or partially funded by the United States. The thrust of all these efforts have always been to strengthen those institutions seen in a positive light by Washington and to enlist support for its policies in the international halls of power.

4- The foreign investment factor

U.S. foreign investments in the area have been rising steadily since their low point in the aftermath of the September 11, 2001 terrorist attacks. Investments were attracted by the stable political environment and well trained and educated labor force. Investments have and continue to be in resort hotel development, financial services, consumer goods distribution and retailing (Home Depot in Saint Lucia, for example) and many offshore outsource industries (electronic parts and computer chips in Saint Kitts and Nevis) that help meet mainland supply needs. These enterprises are generally value-adding and high technology in nature, generating high profits to local business and high returns to foreign investors.

5- Narcotics interdiction

This reason is probably the least rational of all but explains why the United States keeps a vigilant watch over the entire Caribbean region. Washington has long been committed to its "war on drugs." This "war" is being waged on the American mainland and is also being waged in the jungles of South America and in the Caribbean. Aware that some drug trafficking involves the use of air and sea routes from South America via the eastern Caribbean islands to North American markets, it has enlisted the official assistance of local governments to help snuff out the trade. Those efforts at narcotics interdiction have had limited success, but have nevertheless required U.S. assistance that have indirectly benefited local economies in providing jobs and income in the field of law enforcement.

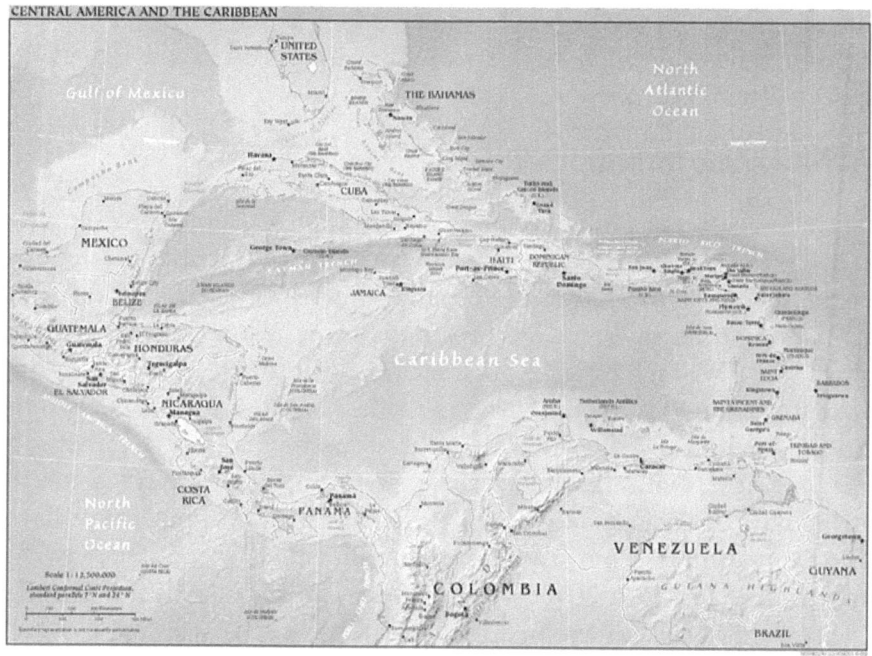

Source: CIA World Fact Book, October, 2008.

4

A Bird's Eye View Of The Region

I- The American Connection

There are few families in the English speaking eastern Caribbean who do not have relatives living in the United States, and the region is well known to residents of the northeastern United States who regularly spend their winter vacations either on cruise ships making the rounds of the islands or in some trendy resort hotel. But to the vacationing tourist, even to returning travelers, the islands become a blur of memories.

And indeed the U.S. departments of State, Defense and Commerce tend to regard the region within the broader context of the entire Caribbean or West Indies for policy purposes. Washington's Caribbean Basin Initiative covers the mainland Central and South American countries facing the Caribbean Sea as well as the Greater and Lesser Antilles. American tourists seeking a vacation destination tend to view the entire region in its entirety first before cherry picking one place to visit, the final decision usually being made on the basis of price and what's "in" or "out" rather than on the merits of its cultural and historical attractions. The Caribbean is a winter destination, and it is the Caribbean's overall safeguarding that is important to U.S. national security and presses mostly in the minds of policy makers in Washington.

The fact that several English speaking eastern Caribbean states have had their economic and political interests lined up with the regional goals of the Organization of East Caribbean States (OECS) has received little attention outside the Caribbean and even less attention in Washington. For example, the United States has only one full service embassy covering the OECS and Barbados, which is not an OECS member, and the embassy is in Barbados. There is a named embassy in Grenada, but its head is a Charge D' Affaires that reports to the American embassy in Bridgetown. [1]

Embassy workers are often dispatched to the other independent OECS states for special missions when required but their authority descends from the Bridgetown facility. In contrast to the absence of a hands-on presence by Washington, other countries like the Chinese, Russians, and Venezuelans are more visible in helping the individual states manage their economic affairs.

The total population of the states covered in this book is about a million. It is easy to dismiss their significance or importance to the United States when one thinks of economies of scale, market size or even market potential. Nor does the region reach the national security radar now that new technologies have reduced the region's strategic military and intelligence importance.

But this is a case where the value of the whole is greater than the sum of its parts. One million people spread over an extensive string of islands may evoke a shrug, but one million people can attract attention when included as part of a much larger region housing a population of 41.5 million. Insofar as U.S. foreign policy is concerned, this diverse expanse of people, land and resources has too often been subject to benign neglect except in periods of emergency that attract the attention of the mainland or seem to threaten the national security. The former English colonies of the eastern Caribbean have especially been ignored by policy makers, and interest in their development has been a more recent result of their rising popularity as tourist destinations.

Once economic backwaters by any measure of performance, several have joined the ranks of high-income nations (Bermuda) and others have become much sought after emerging markets. Most of them are classified as middle income economies (Barbados) and a few, very unfortunately, have stayed poor (Haiti). But rich, middle income or poor, they offer a greater array of opportunities for trade and investments than ever before.

Insofar as American interests are concerned, they are both economic and political. They are economic by virtue of the region's market and investment potential. They are political by virtue of their strategic geographic position in America's war on drugs and by the fact that America cannot afford to be flanked by hostile societies. It is a quid pro quo. America needs friends in the world and the West Indies needs access to American markets and to American financial resources to sustain growth and development. England's former colonies in the eastern Caribbean are especially critical in those two contexts.

The falling apart of Cuban-American relations in the early 1960's is an example of how important it is to maintain functional relationships with every country and territory in the region. A lack of mutuality between Cuba and the United States led to a long period of instability in the Americas that lasted well into the 1990's and has ramifications to this day.

For a variety of reasons the two countries were either unwilling or unable to reach an accommodation and Cuba went on to export, with Russian, its revolution throughout the hemisphere with Che Guevera as its point man. Hence, it was no surprise when he ended up in Bolivia where he was finally trapped and killed. It should have also been no surprise when the Sandinista movement under the leadership of Daniel Ortega prevailed in Nicaragua and turned it into a communist state.

Those events demonstrated the popularity and reach of Cuban power as a proxy for the Soviet Union and its Marxist principles. It can reasonably be argued that this fear by Washington of another foreign policy failure in the Western Hemisphere may have prompted its invasion of Grenada in 1983 when its government went left of center, happening as it did in the aftermath of the fall of Nicaragua's Samoza regime in 1979.

Che Guevera's death in Bolivia represented a Cuban failure but results in Nicaragua have given Washington headaches that exist today. Grenada may have given up its communist leanings, but Venezuela under Hugo Chavez is increasingly flexing its muscles in the Caribbean, vying to replace Cuba as the major leftist power to challenge U.S. influence. .

In terms of business development, many American based companies are today heavily invested in the region and a wealthy, healthy and strong West Indies, including Cuba, its largest and most populous player, is critical not only to U.S. economic enterprise but to its national security. It is therefore important for the region to be considered in terms of its competitive potential, its importance in international affairs and as an equal partner in hemispheric and world affairs. It is even more important in this respect for the West Indies to achieve a greater measure of political and economic integration than it has in the past. A divided West Indies is the greatest threat to itself, to the stability of the Americas and to the national security of the United States.

II- Defining the West Indies as a cultural hegemony

The West Indies is more than that colorful collage of sub-tropical/ tropical lands. It is a cultural hegemony of sovereign nations and semi-autonomous territories in and around the Caribbean Sea that share a common historical background as colonies of the major Western European powers from the sixteenth to twentieth centuries. Much of the West Indies served as in-transit points between European colonizers and the main Western Hemisphere's land mass. All of the West Indies was politically subordinate and subservient to the Western European powers until well into 1900's.

Much has been written about the economics and politics of the slave trade and of the plantation societies that used the sweat, blood and tears of slaves to produce sugar and other commodities. While salient to the region's social, political and economic goals, it is not the central issue of this book. What is more important is how, with the past as background and the present as given, the West Indies, the English speaking eastern Caribbean states included, will continue to grow and produce synergistic results in an equitable interaction with important powers like the United States.

III- The West Indies can be divided into four linguistic groups

If the West Indian heritage is a cultural hegemony, it is not culturally homogenous. It can be divided into four linguistic groups. In descending population numbers, they are: Spanish, French, English and Dutch.

The Spanish West Indies is the largest linguistic group with 24,500,000 people, 11 .3 million living in Cuba. The rest are concentrated in the Dominican Republic and Puerto Rico with 9.3 milliom and 3.9 million respectively.

The next largest grouping is the French West Indies with 9,755,400 people, 8.7 million of which live in Haiti. The third largest grouping is the English speaking West Indies with 6,548,600 people, most of whom reside in Jamaica (2.7 million) and in Trinidad and Tobago (1.050 million) The Dutch speaking West Indies are the smallest grouping with 787,000 people, over half of whom live in Suriname and speak Papamiento, a Creole dialect spoken in Aruba, Bonaire and Curacao.

A- The West Indies is more than the Caribbean [2]

For purposes of this book, the West Indies includes all the islands of the Caribbean but not the countries of Central America despite that fact that they all, with the exceptions of El Salvador and Guatemala, face the Caribbean Sea. The east side of Mexico's Yucatan is also flanked by the Caribbean but Mexico is not classified as a Caribbean or West Indian nation. It will be treated in a separate volume dealing with Latin America along with the countries of Venezuela and Colombia. Belize is in Central America but its cultural ethos is closer to that of English West Indies than to the heritage of Spain's former colonies and is included here as a part of the West Indies. The same rationalization applies to French Guiana, The Co-operative Republic of Guyana (formerly British Guiana) and Suriname (formerly Dutch Guiana). The three "Guianas" are on South America's northern coast on the Atlantic Ocean but are treated as part of the West Indies. Barbados is in the Atlantic east of the Caribbean but is nevertheless included within the West Indies along with the Bahamas, (in the Atlantic north of Cuba), the Turks and Caicos (in the Atlantic north of Cuba and the island Hispaniola (Haiti and the Dominican Republic) and Bermuda, which is several hundreds of miles north in the middle of the Atlantic.

B- The West Indies is larger than the United States [3]

If Bermuda, Belize and the three "Guianas" are included as part of the West Indies, an odd shaped archipelago with mainland appendages begins to take shape. Its north-south range from 33 North Latitude (Bermuda) to 5 North Latitude (French Guiana) is about 1,880 miles. Its east-west range from 88 West Longitude (Belize) to 60 West Longitude (Barbados) is over 3,000 miles. Summarily, the West Indies covers 5,640,000 square miles of much water and little land as opposed to the land mass of the United States which is 3.5 million miles. Its population is almost 42 million, compared to over 305 million for America. [4]

C- The West Indian image

Every person who has ever stayed at a Caribbean resort or visited the area aboard a cruise ship very quickly becomes a self-styled expert on everything West Indian. For the many, the West Indies is a holiday destination that competes for tourist dollars as do so many other warm weather places filled with the mandatory white sandy beaches, the palm trees and the obligatory historical sites and artifacts. Of course the tourist cannot be blamed for this singular image of the West Indies. Indeed, West Indian history is greatly responsible for the somewhat parallel development of many of the societies that emerged in the backwash of colonialism's receding tide. One striking feature has been the area's over-reliance on extractive industries (cash crops like sugar and bananas, and bauxite for aluminum) and tourism. Up to now, many of these pursuits have been foreign oriented and foreign dominated, existing more to benefit the more industrial societies of Europe and America than those of the West Indies.

This is the snapshot often taken away by outsiders who tend to regard the problems faced by one West Indian nation as common to all. This illusion has often proven to be a trap for policy makers and business leaders. The fact remains that countries like Barbados, Dominica, Saint Lucia, Saint Kitts and Grenada face problems unique to each of them, and so it goes with all West Indian countries. That is especially true of the east Caribbean states. Grenada needs more tourism but Barbados could use more high technology industries. [5]

D- Five points of commonality

There are nevertheless four general points of political and economic behavior that are common to the entire region. These have helped determine the direction of individual West Indian government planning, business decision making and even events since the early days of self-government and independence in the 1950's. They have also impacted U.S. foreign policy and business investments with a mix of positive and negative results.

1- Commitment to economic growth and development

The first general point is that most West Indian societies are committed to economic growth and development. To achieve these twin mantras of public policy, it is clear that endogenous and exogenous investments together are seen as components of just about any single growth model selected to reach those objectives.

2- Commitment to regional economic integration

The second general point is that in most West Indian societies (especially in the English speak areas), achieving a level of regional economic integration based on the style of the European Union through organizations like the Caribbean Common Market is a work in progress that has also preoccupied the region since its early days of independence. In any number of ways, that concern has contributed to the region's overall policy architecture of trade and investments. Regional economic integration a la European Union may be a long way off, but efforts to collectively negotiate with the rest of the world are gaining some momentum.

3- The anti-integration spirit

The third general point is that resistance to the goals of regional economic integration is manifesting itself through the counter current of political and economic nationalism. One can understand how cultural divisions based linguistic differences might drive different groups of Caribbean countries to go their different ways, although once sworn enemies like England, France and Germany have succeeded in forging a union of sorts in Europe based upon mutual economic objectives. It is more difficult to comprehend why even the smallest political entities in the West Indies, who happen to be situated in the English speaking eastern Caribbean, resist creating a broader political union.

Two examples stand out. Anguilla, for example, with a population of 14,000 opted out of a union with neighboring islands in favor of maintaining a direct relationship with the United Kingdom. Saint Kitts and Nevis with 43,000 people has for years been contending with a secessionist movement by the residents of Nevis.

And none of the West Indian states, having memberships in common in just about every regional association in the Caribbean that is committed to the region's economic growth, have ever developed mutually cooperative and workable policies and programs to minimize their competition for the same industrial markets. Lack of economic integration and unity of purpose are perhaps the two major obstacles to growth facing those countries today. [6]

4- The direction of trade [7]

The fourth general point of commonality lies in the direction of trade and investments in the individual West Indian states. Although there exists today more intra-regional commerce than ever before, most countries and territories in the region continue to deal principally with the world's major markets. This is quite apparent when the direction of trade of the English speaking eastern Caribbean is examined. Most of what is produced locally is consumed in North America and Europe, and conversely, most of what the region consumes comes from North America, Europe, Asia and larger Caribbean suppliers like Trinidad and Tobago and Venezuela.

5- The emigration issue [8]

Most West Indian emigration (a reason why overall population has grown so little since the mid-1970's when it stood at about 35 million) has been and continues to be to North America and Europe. And finally, most business investments into the region have also been from North America, Europe and more lately from Asia. From this point of view, it is understandable that many West Indian states have become more accustomed to dealing one-on-one with the outside world than as part of a collective whole. This is also true of the English speaking east Caribbean states.

H- Economic growth and development

It is often argued that economic growth and economic development are not the same, and that is probably true. Economic growth can be measured by comparing changes in the average material well being of the individual through periodic changes real per capita income (changes in real gross domestic product per every man, woman and child or per capita GDP).

Economic development addresses the distribution of income that maximizes the well being of all individuals in a society. In this vein, it is also argued that there can be no development without growth; and that probably is true as well. The challenge facing the OECS members are both economic growth and economic development. How the OECS countries address those twin issues will largely determine their long term independence and prosperity.

The 2007-2008 "Global Competitiveness Index" (CGI) published by the World Economic Forum lists rankings for 131 countries for which data is available and verifiable. The CGI considers 113 variables organized into 12 major "pillars" considered critical to successful growth and development. These "pillars" are, according to the World Economic Forum: [9]

1- Institutions	7- Labor market efficiency
2- Infrastructure	8- Financial sophistication
3- Macroeconomic stability	9- Technological readiness
4- Health and primary education	10- Market size
5- Higher education and training	11- Business sophistication
6- Goods market efficiency	12- Innovation

The factors listed above are important to attract business investment, but equally and perhaps even more important is the business investment and all the financial resources it can garner. But business investment is attracted by market size and demand. This is what creates difficulty for the West Indies. Individual states in the region have relatively small populations (Cuba being the largest). Hence their domestic markets are limited and they must look overseas for opportunities. What and how much can be "exported" abroad is a function of the foreign elasticity of demand manifesting itself in the rest of the world for goods and services originating in the West Indies.

For example, Saudi Arabia and the United Arab Emirates are wealthy today because of their energy resources for which world demand is presently high (inelastic) and rising higher as finite supplies try to satisfy infinite demand. Unfortunately, the West Indies has not found much oil. However, it does have bananas, sugar and great weather (tourism). But there are many countries within Cancer and Capricorn with warm weather, attractive tourist attractions and basic food commodities. That creates a situation where prices must be kept sufficiently low to stay competitive and in business.

Insofar as how the West Indies fares on the CGI scale, Puerto Rico is ranked no. 36 and Barbados is ranked no. 50. Jamaica, Trinidad and Tobago and the Dominican Republic are ranked nos. 78, 84 and 96 respectively. One would suspect that other states would fare better (the Bahamas, Bermuda, the Cayman Islands and the Dutch West Indies are cases in point) but they were not included in the survey by the World Economic Forum.

I- Dependency or real independence

Is it important for the West Indies and for the East Caribbean in particular to be a competitive player in the World? The answer to the question is a matter of attitude. Sir Lynden Oscar Pindling, the Bahamian statesman who led his country to independence in 1973, once asked the rhetorical question, "Do we want to be a nation of waiters and bellhops?" [10]

Most of the English speaking east Caribbean states, like much of the West Indies, are today independent or self governing. Yet while their West Indian neighbors trade mostly with the United States and Canada (with the obvious exception of Cuba), Barbados and the OECS states have a mixed pattern of merchandise trade. Their goods exports are generally purchased by the high income countries of North America and Europe, but their imports come from both North American, European and Asian industrial countries and emerging markets elsewhere in the Caribbean and South America like Trinidad and Tobago and Venezuela.

The OECS region is also less beholden to its history and roots. Much of this has been a result of a static and/or declining population growth due in large part to emigration. About 6% of first and second generation American residents have family connections in the West Indies, a relationship that impacts urban political and social relations and of course policy decisions. For example, more Grenadians and Montserratians live in other countries than in Grenada or Montserrat.

5

The West Indies At A Glance

I- Chapter Layout

This study is organized around the nine OECS states and Barbados. It is however relevant at this time, since they form part of a greater whole, to take a bird's eye view of the entire West Indies to whose family they belong. The reader is invited to use the map of the Caribbean in Table II to have a better idea of exactly where the individual West Indian states are located.

Most of the West Indies lie in the Caribbean Sea or along its peripheries. Those outside are: the Bermuda Islands, the Bahamas, the Turks and Caicos, Barbados, Belize (Formerly British Honduras), and the three Guianas on the northern coast of South America (Guyana, Suriname and French Guiana).

The Bermuda Islands are situated past the northern edge of the Sargasso Sea in the Atlantic Ocean about 500 miles due east of Charleston, South Carolina. The Bahamas and the Turks and Caicos are east of the Florida Straits and north of Cuba and Hispaniola and are also in the Atlantic, as is Barbados which is east of the Windward Islands. Belize, on the Central American mainland, faces the Caribbean, and the three Guianas face the Atlantic on South America's northern coast.

The Greater Antilles, Cuba, Hispaniola (housing Haiti and the Dominican Republic) and Puerto Rico face the Atlantic to the north and the Caribbean Sea to the south. The Lesser Antilles (the

Leeward and Windward Islands) extend southeasterly from Puerto Rico southeast to Dominica and then curve to the southwest from Martinique to Grenada.

The OECS states are spread over both island groups. Anguilla, Antigua, Saint Kitts and Nevis, Montserrat and Dominica are in the Leeward Islands, while Saint Lucia, Saint Vincent and Grenada are in the Windward Islands. Barbados is in the middle of the Atlantic ocean about 100 miles east of Saint Lucia and Saint Vincent.

The non-English speaking states in the eastern Caribbean are Guadeloupe, Martinique, Saint Barts, Saba and Saint Marten/Saint Martin and a number of smaller satellite islands. The non-English speaking islands in the southern Caribbean are Aruba, Bonaire and Curacao.

Trinidad and Tobago, also in the southern Caribbean, is English speaking, but is not included in this study since it is not an OECS member. The U.S. Virgin Islands and U.K. Virgin Islands are in the Leeward Islands group and are included in this book.

The next part of this chapter offers a summary glimpse of the individual states' basic data: political status, population, per capita GDP and longevity. The last part of the chapter briefly summarizes each state's political and economic environment.

II- Quick Facts and Figures*

State	Population	Per Capita GDP	Life Span	HDI*	HDI Rank **
Anguilla	13,000	8,800	70		
Antigua	70,000	11,000	70	0.815	57
Aruba	112,000	22,000	78		
Bahamas	275,000	21,600	65	0.845	49
Barbados	280,000	18,400	73	0.892	31
Belize	300,000	8,500	68	0.778	80
Bermuda	66,000	75,500	78		
Bonaire	16,000	22,000	78		

Caymans	47,000	30,000	78		
Cuba	11,300.00	4,000	77	0.838	51
Curacao	138,000	18,000	78		
Dominica	73,000	3,800	75	0.798	71
Dominican Republic	9,300,000	8,400	73	0.779	79
French Guiana	203,000	18,000	77		
Grenada	90,000	2,900	65	0.777	82
Guadeloupe	408,000	22,000	77		
Guyana	770,000	4,800	66	0.75	97
Haiti	8,710,000	1,800	57	0.529	146
Jamaica	2,700,000	4,600	73	0.736	101
Martinique	401,000	22,000	77		
Montserrat	12,000				
Puerto Rico	3,900,000	13,000	78		
St. Barts	8,400	30,000	78		
St. Martin	35,000	30,000	78		
St. Marten	50,000	30,000	78		
St. Kitts/Nevis	43,000	15,000	75	0.821	54
St. Lucia	171,000	4,800	74	0.795	72
St. Vincent	119,000	3,600	74	0.761	93
Suriname	271,000	7,100	73	0.774	85
Trinidad	1,050,000	20,000	66	0.814	59
Turks/Caicos	25,000	20,000	75		
Virgin Islands UK	22,000	20,000	75		
Virgin Islands US	108,000	20,000	75		

* The Human Development Index (HDI), published by the World Bank in its 2007-2008 Human Development Report is based on a mix of index numbers covering the following factors: life expectancy at birth, adult literacy rate and the combined gross enrolment ratio for all levels of education and GDP per capita. The indices derived are: life expectancy, education and GDP. For Barbados as an example, its life expectancy index is 0.861, its education index is 0.956, and its GDP index is 0.860. The rankings range from No. 1 (Iceland) to No. 177 (Sierra Leone). Barbados for example is ranked No. 37 while Jamaica is ranked No. 100 and Haiti is ranked No. 149. The USA is ranked No. 13 with a score of) 0.956. Its 2010 population is about 310 million and its per capita GDP is about $40,000. No HDI data available for non-sovereign territories.

III- The West Indies at a glance (See note at the end of the Chapter)*

1- Anguilla. This cluster of small islands is part of the British West Indies that forms a large crescent from the Turks and Caicos (east of the Bahamas and north of Hispaniola) to the British Virgin Islands (due east of the U.S. Virgin islands) and then south to Monserrat and finally east to the Caymans (due south of Cuba). Anguilla is the most northern island of the Leeward group in the Lesser Antilles that includes the U.K. and U.S. Virgins, and Montserrat. Although these islands are technically self-governing, they are political dependencies of the United Kingdom. The principal contributors to the area's gross domestic product are fishing, agriculture, tourism and financial services. Drug trafficking is reported having a role in the Turks and Caicos. High-end boutique tourism is the mainstay of Anguilla's economy as it tries to compete with expensive resort destinations like St. Barts further to the south.

2- Antigua. This island is situated in the Leeward group of the Lesser Antilles and is actually part of a two-island group, Antigua and Barbuda with whom are associated four minor cays, Guiana Island, Great Bird Island, Lesser Bird Island, Prickly Pear island and Redonda. It is fully independent but it does recognize the English crown as its nominal head of state. Principal contributors to Antigua's gross domestic product are some limited manufacturing, fishing, agriculture, tourism and financial services. However, financial services and tourism are not as highly developed as in other islands such as St. Marten (Dutch), the Bahamas (Independent), Bermuda (English) and Aruba (Dutch).

3- Aruba. This island, off the northern coast of South America (facing Venezuela) and its neighboring cays, is part of the Netherlands Antilles (Bonaire, Curacao, Saint Marten, Saint Eustatius and Saba). However, Aruba separated itself from the Netherlands West Indies (a political association) in 1986. It continues to be an autonomous member of the Netherlands, the same status accorded to the other former Dutch colonies. Aruba is a major tourist destination and naturally the tourism industry dominates its economy. It is one of the richest of West Indian islands in terms of per capita income. It has in many respects become the "Las Vegas" of the Caribbean.

4- The Bahamas. There are 700 islands in this national archipelago that extends like a string of pearls from a point about 100 miles east of Palm Beach to the Turks and Caicos north of Hispaniola in the Atlantic Ocean. Independent from the United Kingdom since 1973, it is governed by a prime minister and an elected legislative assembly based on a system of proportional representation. Main economic contributors are fishing, limited agriculture, very limited manufacturing, tourism and financial services. However, tourism and financial services contribute to over 70% of the country's gross domestic product. It is reported that the Bahamas is a major transit point for the trafficking of drugs to Florida.

5- Barbados. This island is east of the Windward Islands in the Atlantic Ocean and not in the Caribbean. Independent from the United Kingdom since 1973, it is a parliamentary democracy governed by a prime minister and an elected legislative assembly based on a system of proportional representation. Its main economic activities are agriculture, light manufacturing and tourism. Casino hotel tourism is not allowed in Barbados and that may be a reason why its economy, although quite developed, lags behind those who do permit organized gambling.

6- Belize. This country lies on the Central American mainland facing the Caribbean. It was known as British Honduras until it became an independent nation in 1981. It is a parliamentary democracy governed by a prime minister selected by the political party in power. Its nominal head of state is a governor-general representing the English crown. Its main economic activities are light manufacturing, tourism and agriculture. The country is said to be sitting on 6.7 million barrels of crude oil reserves. It is also reported to have become an important transit point for the trafficking of drugs between Colombia and the United States. It is believed that an underground economy based on drug trafficking is thriving.

7- Bermuda. This is a British dependency in the Atlantic Ocean encompassing more than 150 coral islands of which about 20 are inhabited. It is ruled by a royal governor who presides over a locally elected assembly, a system in place since 1620. Its main economic occupations are off-shore financial and insurance services and tourism. Compact size and a small, highly educated population along with a very close relationship with England and the United States have helped turn it into the richest political unit in the Western Hemisphere.

8- Bonaire. This island, east of Curacao off the northern coast of South America (facing Venezuela) and with a population of about 16,000, is closely linked to Curacao with the Netherlands West Indies. It has a parliamentary government and its key industry is water sports tourism. It has considerable salt deposits but that industry is not as important as it once was. Bonaire's economy, by design, is not as developed as in Curacao and Aruba.

Its cardinal feature is a dedication to "sustainable" development in order to preserve the island's natural habitat.

9- Caymans. There are three islands, Grand Cayman, Little Cayman and Cayman Brac, sit under Cuba and are British dependencies. There is some fishing and limited manufacturing, but the main economic activities are financial services and tourism.

10- Cuba. This country is a republic based on a single-party government featuring a centrally planned economy. Economic activity is diversified but relatively unproductive due to internal and international political conditions.

11- Curacao. This island, off the northern coast of South America (facing Venezuela), is an integral part of the Netherlands West Indies with a good measure of self-governing status. Tourism is important to the island but not as important as oil refining, its main source of income and wealth. Curacao is governed by an elected legislature presided over by a lieutenant governor appointed by the Dutch crown.

12- Dominica. This island is part of the Windward Islands in the Lesser Antilles. It is a parliamentary democracy with a president as head of state and a prime minister as the head of government. Its economy is basically agricultural with some light manufacturing. It has lately been trying to develop its tourism industry.

13- Dominican Republic. This country is a republic and occupies the eastern two thirds of the island of Hispaniola in the Greater Antilles. It has been independent since the 1860's. It has an elected president and a legislature elected on the basis of proportional representation. The main contributors to its gross domestic product are agriculture and light manufacturing. Tourism is a growing industry.

14- French Guiana. On the northeast coast of South America facing the Atlantic Ocean, it is one of France's overseas departments, meaning that residents of French Guiana are citizens of France. Once a penal colony (Devil's Island), the territory's main activities today are fishing, forestry and gold mining.

15- Grenada. This island forms part of the Windward Islands group in the Lesser Antilles. It is a parliamentary democracy with the British crown as the nominal head of state. The head of government is an elected prime minister who presides over an elected legislature. The mainstays of its economy are agriculture, light assembly and manufacturing and a small but growing tourism industry.

16- Guadeloupe. This island straddles the Leeward and Windward Islands group in the Lesser Antilles, Guadeloupe is one of France's overseas departments, meaning that it residents are citizens of France. Its main economic activities are agriculture, fishing and some tourism.

17- Guyana. On the northeast coast of South America facing the Atlantic Ocean, it was formerly known as British Guyana until its independence in 1966. It is a republic and is organized as a parliamentary democracy with a president and legislature. The mainstays of its economy are agriculture, forestry mining (bauxite, gold and diamonds).

18- Haiti. This country occupies the western third of the island of Hispaniola which is part of the Greater Antilles. The eastern two thirds of Hispaniola is occupied by the Dominican Republic. Haiti is a republic with a president. Its main economic occupations are agriculture, mining (bauxite, copper, calcium carbonate and some marble and gold) and light manufacturing. Tourism is limited by the country's political instability.

19- Jamaica. The country, lying south of Cuba, is part of the Greater Antilles. It is a parliamentary democracy whose head of state is the British crown, represented by a governor-general. The head of government is a prime minister presiding over an elected legislature. Its principal economic pursuits are agriculture, mining (bauxite), food and chemical processing, financial services and tourism. It is reported to be a major drug trafficking center.

20- Martinique. Part of the Windward Islands group in the Lesser Antilles, It is an overseas department of France, and its residents are citizens of France. Its main economic output is fishing, agriculture and some tourism.

21- Montserrat. Part of the Leeward Islands group in the Lesser Antilles, it is part of the British West Indies. It was devastated by a volcanic eruption in the 1990's and has yet to fully recover.

22- Puerto Rico. This island forms part of the Greater Antilles and sits directly east of the Dominican Republic. It is a commonwealth and is part of the United States, having been taken from Spain during the Spanish American War in 1898. It has an elected governor that presides over an elected legislature. Its economy is diversified and has a strong agricultural and manufacturing base. It also has a strong tourism sector.

23- St. Barts. Considered part of France's overseas departments, it is part of the Leeward Islands in the Lesser Antilles. Agriculture and fishing are the mainstays of its economy.

A small but growing tourism industry is beginning to contribute to re-shape the economy.

24- St. Martin. This territory is an overseas department of France and its residents are French citizens. It occupies the northern part of a small island in the Leeward Islands group of the Lesser Antilles. The island's southern portion is called St. Marten and is part of the Netherlands West Indies. Somewhat more rural but as developed as its southern counterpart, tourism is its major industry.

25- St. Marten. This territory occupies the southern part of the island mentioned above and is part of the Netherlands West Indies. Like its northern counterpart, tourism is the industry driving its economy. Like Aruba, it is a major destination for tourists coming from the eastern United States and Canada.

26- St Kitts and Nevis. These two islands are in the Leeward Islands group of the Lesser Antilles. It is independent and the nominal head of state is the British crown. A prime minister is head of government and presides over a legislative assembly representing 14 political parishes from the two islands. Its economy is driven by tourism and agriculture. An interesting historical note is that Alexander Hamilton was born in Nevis.

27- St. Lucia. This island is in the Windward Islands group of the Lesser Antilles. Its head of state is the British crown and its head of government is a prime minister that presides over a legislature. Main economic contributors are light manufacturing, agriculture and tourism.

28- St. Vincent. This island is in the Windward group in the Lesser Antilles and, together with a chain of smaller islands known as the Grenadines, is a single independent country. Agriculture and fishing are the mainstays of its economy.

29- Suriname. Once known as Dutch Guiana and situated on the northeast coast of South America facing the Atlantic Ocean, it has been independent since 1975. The head of state and head of government is an elected president presiding over a legislature. Agriculture, fishing, forestry and mining (bauxite, copper, gold, iron ore, nickel and platinum) support the economy. It has been reported that the country has crude oil reserves in the amount of 111 million barrels.

30- Trinidad & Tobago. This two-island country sits off the northern coast of South America (facing Venezuela). It gained independence in 1962 and turned itself into a republic in 1976. It has an industrial, diversified economy driven largely by its position as a chemical and petroleum refining and processing center. It is a major producer of asphalt and sits on 728 million barrels of crude oil reserves.

31- Turks & Caicos. This string of islands, like the rest of the British West Indies is one of England's political dependencies, and lies due east of the Bahamas and north of the island of Hispaniola. A supplier of salt to Bermuda in centuries past, the mainstays of its economy today are financial services and tourism. Back in the 1990's one of its government ministers was arrested in Florida and convicted of drug dealing.

32- Virgin Islands (British). About fifty islands make up this dependency of the United Kingdom which are east of the U.S. Virgin Islands The largest is the island of Tortola. The three mainstays of its economy are financial services and tourism and the retail/wholesale trade they bring.

33- Virgin Islands (U.S.). Three islands and their adjacent cays make up this group, St. Croix, St. John and St. Thomas. They lie east of Puerto Rico and the islands of Culebra and Vieques (which belong to Puerto Rico). They are a self-governing dependency of the United States with their own elected governor and legislature. Residents are citizens of the U.S. The economic mainstays of the islands are tourism and the considerable retail/wholesale trade that results.

* The information above is from the CIA World Fact Book on the web (cia.org/library) accessed in October, 2009.

6

Historical Environments

I- Background: the West Indian Enigma

A- Pre-Colombian societies were not long distance maritime explorers

It is difficult to deny that observation that pre-Columbian societies in the Western hemisphere were easy prey for the European invaders and that in the Caribbean specifically, issues of political control superseded conquest. It seems now clear that local societies had neither the interest nor the skills to engage in long distance explorations and wars. No evidence exists to date of any exploration, discovery and colonization by its indigenous inhabitants of other lands beyond those of the Western Hemisphere. Accepting the validity of the claim that its inhabitants originally came from Asia and developed sophisticated civilizations, it is odd that normal curiosity and acquisitiveness did not encourage more adventurous types to eventually seek new horizons beyond the sea. If this pursuit of seafaring adventure was absent, so lacking were the maritime and military technologies needed for launching repeated expeditions over vast stretches of open water to explore, conquer and occupy new lands.

B- Early Migrations [1]

Over-water migrations did take place, however. It is thought, for instance, that Hawaii's early settlers came from either Asia, the South

Pacific islands or from the Western Hemisphere's mainland. It is also fairly well established that the islands of the Caribbean Sea were originally settled by immigration from Central and South America and maybe even from the south eastern United States. The Arawaks arrived in the Caribbean from the mainland on ocean going canoes. So later did the Caribs whose long war canoes harassed European shipping until the end of the 1700's.

This suggests that their navigational skills and knowledge of the stars and sea were equal to that of their European foes. Why these intrepid people, and even Native Americans in North America living along coastal areas, did not pursue opportunities to develop or adopt the available know-how of the day to follow prevailing winds and currents up the coast and then northeast under Labrador, Greenland, Iceland and finally to Europe remains a mystery.

C- Invention and technology

Although these pre-Colombian societies never seemed to have bothered with traveling far beyond their immediate water-bound horizons, there exists archeological and anthropological evidence indicating that their theoretical and applied knowledge was similar to those of European and Asian cultures at the time of contact. What appeared to have been different was context and purpose, and the lack of firearms.

The wheel, for example, existed in fact and concept in the pre-Colombian societies funneling down the Central American chute into South America, but its use was confined to ceremonial functions and toys. Knowledge of the position and movement of celestial bodies was also widespread, but practical applications of celestial navigation to maritime travel were never attempted except for short voyages.

Boats were in common usage for local fishing and transport, but this know how never developed into a trans-ocean maritime tradition. Nor was there a recorded attempt to mass produce larger, seaworthy boats to move armies of people and large quantities of supplies on long voyages over ocean waters to faraway destinations.

II- Interesting Historical Trivia

A- The global reach of ancient worlds [2]

When one examines those ancient cultures on the Eurasian continent that grew along coastlines, a different mindset emerges. Navies from China and the Indian subcontinent had been prowling Asian waters for commerce and conquest for thousands of years. Ancient Egyptian, Greek and Phoenician civilizations had naval and merchant fleets to cover the Mediterranean Sea thousands of years before the Christian era, and by the time of the Roman era, achieving naval supremacy had become a cardinal goal of state military policy to control North African and European waters beyond Gibraltar.

Ancient Eurasian civilizations also had a reasonably sound geographic knowledge that was partly based on mathematics and philosophy. Pythagoras, in the sixth century B.C., noted that the world was a globe. While it is true that he had no real evidence upon which to rest his ideas, his claim that the world was round stemmed from the hypothesis that a sphere was a perfect form and was therefore the center of the universe. His conclusion, certainly flawed, ended up being the basis for all future discourse concerning the world's geography.

Aristotle (384-322 BCE) accepted the Pythagorean hypothesis which was further refined by Ptolemy in the second century CE. His work dominated thinking about the universe and the world until the fifteenth century when empirical knowledge about the known world expanded enough to expose the flaws in the reasoning of the Ancients. By then the concept of the world as being round had moved from the realms of philosophy and mathematics to practical reality. The questions left to be answered in the half century before Christopher Columbus's historic voyage related principally to the earth's circumference and to what lands might exist if any in the waters separating Europe from Asia.

B- Underestimating the Earth's diameter [3]

The error originally made by the ancients was to underestimate the earth's circumference by about three thousand miles. Ptolemy believed the earth's major landmass extended continuously from its western to eastern edges (the so-called Eurasian land mass) and that an enormously wide body of water flowed between those two edges. It was assumed that a few islands yet to be discovered and identified might lie between Europe and Asia, but the idea that a major land barrier that extended from the Arctic to the Antarctic did not exist. Hence, when Europeans in the fourteenth century began seriously to contemplate sailing west to find Asia the prevailing wisdom was that one month's time would carry them directly to Asia's outlying islands, namely Japan.

That was the assumption that Christopher Columbus operated under when he started planning his first voyage. His intention was never to find "a new world" but to navigate an ocean route to Asia as an alternative to the longer and more hazardous overland west to east journey, the itinerary pioneered by Marco Polo two centuries earlier. Indeed, it took him almost three years to make the return trip from Beijing to Venice. Europeans were acquainted with passages to China via the Indian Ocean but their access was blocked by Islamic empires that reigned over the Middle East and were rapidly spreading east to India and the East Indies.

C-Trade routes

Maritime routes for military and commercial purposes began expanding long before the Roman era. Phoenician and Greek fleets began exploring the Atlantic coast regions of North Africa and the Iberian Peninsula before the Homeric age. According to Cyrus Gordon, at around 600 B.C., a ship with a combined crew of Hebrew and Phoenician sailors made its way down the east coast of Africa, rounded the Cape of Good Horn and headed west to South America where a settlement was said to have been attempted in Brazil. It is also pretty well documented that by 300 B.C. the Phoenicians had established lasting trade routes from the Atlantic coast of North Africa, reaching the Azores and the Canary islands, to western England. Roman ships are said to have reached as far north as Iceland in Atlantic at about the same time, and by 500 A.D., active trade routes connected Mediterranean communities to Northern Europe.

Neither were Islamic Arabs idle. By 1000 A.D., Arab merchant fleets had reached India and Indonesia where they established permanent trading centers that were to become the springboards of

Islamic expansion into South Asia. Southbound, they reached Zanzibar (Mozambique) in Africa where they planted permanent settlements.

Northern Europeans were routinely exploring the Western Hemisphere's north eastern coast by 1000 A.D. and by 1200 A.D., permanent settlements existed, complete with Christian churches, in Greenland and Newfound Land. However, a legendary expedition took place about three centuries before. According to the story, a band of survivors from the Moors' invasion of Spain sailed west and settled in an island later called "Antilla" that was later said to have been derived from two Portuguese words, "ante" (against) and "ilha" (island).

The legend's current implication is that the island was located opposite to larger land mass. The story was basically rumor, but what is clear is that the Portuguese in the early 1400's made several voyages west of the Canary islands in attempts to find "Antilla." Although those trips ended without success, the name "Antille" soon found its way to cartographers' charts within a few years of Columbus's crossing in 1492. Today, most of the islands in the Caribbean are described as being either in the "Greater Antilles" or in the "Lesser Antilles."

D- Population in the pre-Columbian Western Hemisphere

An enduring issue revolves around the size of native populations in the Americas in the dawn of the European incursions. It had been believed for many years that the Western Hemisphere was sparsely populated when the Spaniards appeared on the scene. However, low population density is a relative term. Compared to the much smaller European land mass, the geographic vastness of the hemisphere would have easily swallowed Europe's population in 1500 which is estimated to have been about 150 million. Recent studies now suggest that roughly about that same number of people lived in the New World. It is also interesting to note that the estimated world population for 1500 is given at roughly 600 million. With 300 million in Europe and the New World combined, that would have left 120 million in Africa and 200 million in Asia and elsewhere. This data conforms to earlier estimates for Africa and Asia.

Insofar as the West Indies are concerned, the same estimates hypothesize that about ten percent of New World inhabitants, or about 15 million people, lived in the islands except in Bermuda which remained uninhabited until the Europeans discovered the tiny chain. Today, Latin America's population is about 420 million, over 460 million if the West Indies is included.

E-Pre-Columbian migrations

When did New World people first inhabit the West Indies? Estimates vary with little agreement on a particular time frame. Nor is there a consensus as to when the Western Hemisphere was first settled by humans. Until expert archeological discoveries prove otherwise, current theories indicate that the first immigrants began filtering into the hemisphere from Asia about 35,000 to 40,000 years ago. This means that, given the logistics of the age, the first mainland arrivals to the offshore islands could have been between 4,000 and 5,000 years ago. This point will be explained below later.

It is suggested that the first arrivals came from Asia via a sea-land route connecting Siberia to Alaska. While that theory has been disputed, it has never been refuted. Other theories suggest that the first humans crossed the Pacific Ocean from Asia over a land bridge from Asia. That theory too has been disputed, and experiments attempting to replicate the long voyage over open water with technology of the day have been inconclusive.

A third theory set, more recently advanced by Native Americans, argues that humans lived in the Western Hemisphere for hundreds of thousands of years. Evidence supporting this position has also been lacking to date.

Assuming that the overland migration hypothesis is correct, it is then suggested that migrations began from Asia only after human longevity had increased and humans had learned to adapt to the punishing climates found in arctic and sub arctic lands. Even if migrations took place between the late Spring and late Summer, the first migrations would have taken place within the time frame when homo sapiens first learned to wear outer garments that could protect them from the elements. That would have been within the last 30,000 years.

This raises two issues: human life span and the physical distance that could be covered annually on foot by migrants consisting of families, clans, tribes and even larger groups traveling together. Human life span would obviously be the independent factor with the length of the annual migration period as the dependent variable. The distance to be covered was fixed, depending on where people finally staked out permanent settlements; hence, the reason for human longevity as the key.

In general, a group of people could average no more than 400 miles a year, allowing for bad weather, natural calamities, unknown geography, disease and local warfare. Thus, a band of several dozen families or clans embarking on a trek and following game herds needed to provide sustenance while on the move, would take ten years to travel 4,000 miles, or twenty years to move 8,000 miles from Siberia to San Francisco, under ideal conditions. If the average life span of humans was 20 years, the first migrant generation would have had to create a succeeding generation to complete the trip. This would have allowed time for hunting, fishing, giving birth and managing the daily issues of life and death.

The speed of migration and the extent of population dispersion throughout North and South America and subsequently to the West Indies therefore depended mainly on how long people lived and the ability of families to reproduce in transit until they decided to stop considered ripe for settlement. The problem is that almost no records exist that shed light on human birth rates, health and mobility in pre-historic times.

This is why it is unclear whether migration into the Western Hemisphere began as early as 50,000 years ago or as late as 15,000 years ago. If people lived up to thirty years, the migrations could have started later. But if human life span was only twenty years, then migrations would have started closer to 50,000 years ago in order to produce the population numbers that were said to be in place by 1500.

F- Migrations within the Western Hemisphere

Once the migrations started, human movement within the hemisphere seemed to have accelerated. It is estimated that between ten and twelve thousand years ago, the entire region from the polar north to the southern tip of South America was populated with varying degrees of density.

It is probable that the Asian migrations ended about ten thousand years ago as the northern west-to-east route changed geologically.

The rapid receding of glacial ice from the previous ice age gradually increased ocean water levels and submerged the land bridge that is said to have once existed and may have had much to do with bringing the Asian migrations to a halt.

The general thinking today is that the early migrants pushed south of the snow line and that the first permanent settlements may have been in Mexico and in the Southern United States. A counter migration may have occurred as the glacial belt receded so that people identified today as North American Indians may actually not be the direct descendants of southbound migrants but the offspring of those who were already living in geographically defined communities further south.

Whatever the truth may be, a critical fact is that geographic realities most likely shaped the ways of life in the hemisphere found by the Europeans. In general, North American Indians were less sedentary than their neighbors to the south except for tribes in coastal regions. South of the United States, the upper hour glass shape of Mexico and Central America, very wide at the Rio Grande River and very narrow in Panama, required living at close quarters in habitable areas defined by fixed communities within reach of arable land.

In South America, communities thrived around the Andes Mountains with smaller groups spreading east to the lowland jungles in the north and to the plains further south. It is suspected that urban societies surrounded by large agricultural tracts had taken root in Mexico and in Ecuador and Peru to form the cradle from which the Indian empires faced by the Spanish sprang. This culture was exported to the West Indies when mainland Indians began to fan out across the Caribbean. It is also believed that migrations from Central and South America began at that time.

The conventional wisdom is that early arrivals in the West Indies crossed the Gulf of Mexico and the Caribbean Sea directly to the islands. However, that would have required technology that may not have been yet in existence in the hemisphere.

Coastal cruising in smaller canoe shaped vessels equipped with outriggers could have accelerated north-to-south passages by puddle-jumping from point to point, but much larger vessels with deeper hulls and ballasted keels would have been needed for serious, long distance blue water transport. Arguments have also been made that Indians may have crossed over to the islands from Florida. The Biminis, for example, are a tiny cluster of islands a mere forty five miles to the east, and the other major Bahamian islands are scarcely more than one hundred miles away.

The problem with that thesis is that the prevailing winds blow from the east and the Gulf Stream current moves rapidly in a northern direction. Boats leaving from Florida would have easily been blown off course and pushed back to the mainland in simple canoes, whatever their size. Passages from Georgia, the Carolinas and Virginia would have been possible but again those would have required stronger and larger vessels and crews capable of negotiating long stretches of open water.

It is more reasonable to suppose that the first West Indians, the Arawaks and the Caribs, left from northern South America and island hopped their way north through the Lesser Antilles and then headed east-to-west across the Greater Antilles to enjoy both the wind and currents moving their way.

Nevertheless, no matter what course they did take, by 1492, a civilization engaged in small scale agriculture, fishing and inter-island trade was thriving in most of the Caribbean islands.

7

The Colonial Political and Economic Legacy [1]

I- What's in a name?

The collision course set by the Europeans as the 1400's ended proved to be fatal for the cultures of the Western Hemisphere. It was not that Europeans knew much about what was going on some three thousand miles to the west of them; they didn't, and neither did they care. They sailed West with a sort of evangelical zeal and cultural smugness to fulfill a mission of conquest for "God, King and Country" in which the target was at first Asia before finding that another huge land mass lay in their way. But no problem; this new land presented not an obstacle but a challenge and opportunity for conquest and fortune over the hides of indigenous inhabitants who were never considered the equal of the European invaders.

Therefore, the past was violently wiped out to make way for the new and fresh names were assigned to old territories. The terms "Antilles," "Indies," and "West Indies" were appellations coined by European travelers and cartographers to define the South Asian mainland and a chain of islands further east ever since the days of Marco Polo. And hence, the "discoveries" of Christopher Columbus and his followers very quickly came to be known as the "East Indies." Indeed, by the time he was born, the name "Indies" was in fairly common use by European geographers and policy makers. [2]

A crew member on the first voyage of Christopher Columbus in 1492 kept a journal or log in which he often referred to the "Indies," to "Indians" and to the "Carib," an local tribe described in error as cannibals who "eat human flesh." [3] In 1494, the rulers of Spain bestowed on Columbus the title of "High Admiral of the Islands of the Indies." [4]

A- Christopher Columbus's lucky miscalculation

Columbus fully expected that a one month sail west across the ocean from the Canaries would bring him to the Indies. This expectation was based on the knowledge that sailing ships could average about one hundred miles in a twenty four day. This meant that a well found and fully stocked sailing vessel could cover a distance of three thousand miles in a month over open water, enough to reach Asia. He knew that a land mass lay somewhere to the northwest but the course he laid out was intended to pass under it far to the south. [5]

The fact that he came upon some islands along the way to expose a new world simply redrew the map of the world to pave the way for Europeans to a fast conquest and the obliteration of an entire civilization.

B- The seven seeds of destruction

It can be argued that the ultimate downfall of native cultures was due to economic forces that created a momentum that even the Europeans, although up to the challenge technologically, never fully grasped. The one thing they understood was that they possessed overwhelming power and were disposed to use that power to see where it would get them and what rewards were in store. They were, to forgive an over worn term, great risk takers. In the end, it was a clash of cultures based on seven points of economic behavior, each philosophically perceived differently by the two antagonists, that drove the native cultures from power. Native cultures failed because they could never comprehend the emerging European way of life and hence they could never accept it and could never compete.

These seven points of economic behavior can be summarized as follows:

1- Europe had developed foundations of modern capitalist economic and financial enterprise by the beginning of 1400. Indians had only a rudimentary barter system, goods for goods and/or goods for services.

2- Emerging European kingdoms were in the process of creating monetary systems linked to international trade practices in which the need for gold or silver was seen as the key to national prosperity. Such systems never appeared among pre-Columbian cultures.

3- The economic organization of European agriculture was tailor made for the export of the plantation system through foreign colonization. Sugar was a major commodity being produced in the Mediterranean, but continuing conflict with Islamic states threatened its sources of supply. The time was therefore ripe for replicating the industry elsewhere. In the New World, there were indications that the civilizations that once dominated the Western Hemisphere were already in decline by the 1400's.

4- Intensive labor was needed for a plantation system (sugar) and for mining (gold). The European slave trade with Africa began growing in the Middle Ages, but when Columbus reached the West Indies he promptly reported that "One Indian is worth three Negroes." Indians had no economic theory that attempted to define human value and to link it with economic output.

5- The reserve manpower for European colonial expansion to the New World exited through the African slave trade so that when local Indian populations were decimated, they could easily be replaced by Africans. Slavery existed in various forms among the cultures of the West Indies and the Americas, but it never reached the organizational sophistication that was achieved among Europeans.

6- The Spanish, Portuguese, and later the French, Dutch and English were intellectually prepared for new conquests over the sea. Growing scientific and empirical knowledge of the world desired it and Church doctrine demanded it. No similar philosophy existed in the New World to galvanize entire populations to a single purpose.

7- Finally, four revolutionary new technologies evolved in Europe simultaneously: the compass, the printing press, gun powder and firearms and breakthroughs in naval architecture. The invention of the compass made it possible to navigate under starless and sunless skies.

The printing press accelerated communications and made information available to many people at once. The availability of gun powder and firearms provided immediate military superiority over those who had none, and the ability to build larger sailing ships made it possible to move large numbers of people and material. Competitive technologies in general were lacking in the New World.

It could therefore be no surprise that once the Spanish arrived in the West Indies and later in the Americas, it sealed the fate of the Indians.

C- The economic backwater syndrome

The fact that permanent settlements took root in the West Indies before they did on the Western Hemisphere's mainland does not alter the truth that within three centuries of their discovery they were reduced to economic and political backwaters, caught between larger struggles and movements among more powerful players in the world. Europeans who made their inroads first in the West Indies, originally had great plans for the islands they discovered and conquered. The University of Santo Domingo opened its doors in the Dominican Republic in 1511, less than twenty years after Christopher Columbus made his historic voyage. And fortified cities, colonized by thousands of Europeans (mainly Spaniards at first) lured by rumors of gold, began springing up in the West Indies as part of a master plan to turn the region into an integral part of the Spanish Empire's political geography even before Columbus had completed his explorations.

It took only a few decades for Spain and its other European competitors to realize that little gold to be found in the islands and that better opportunities lay on the mainland. By the middle of the 1500's, the West Indies were rapidly being turned into way stations to transport the treasures of Central and South America to Europe.

This change in policy had serious ramifications for the islands. Forced to become self sufficient, the region turned to the slave trade and to a plantation economy to augment its declining way station income.

That was unfortunate for the West Indies because the region never had the opportunity to participate in Europe's economic renaissance and industrial revolution that was to change the face of a good part of the world between 1600 and today. To make matters worse, the elimination of slavery in the 19ᵗʰ century created a new class of poor people who were left without a secure source of income except from what was available through plantation employment and from marginal family farms. That extended a legacy of widespread lingering poverty to the mid 1900's.

When the second half of the twentieth century dawned, it became obvious that even agriculture could not ensure sustainable growth and development, leaving the newly emerging countries of the West Indies to rely on mining, processing industries, the emerging tourist trade and financial services.

The problem with all these economic endeavors was that they were geared to the needs of much larger industrial nations, leaving their survival and growth too dependent upon foreign markets. Hence, aggregate economic growth and development in the region was driven exogenously and scarcely affected by local demand. In a sense, the old colonial legacy of economic and political dependency had survived past the immediate post colonial era of the 1960's and 1970's, past the so-called "development generation" of the 1980's and 1990's and into the current century. Colonialism has thus proven to be a hangover hard to cure.

The enslavement of non-European, non-white populations, the exclusive economic reliance on extractive, commodity type industries, the absence of a critical mass of human resources large enough and with diversified value-adding skills to develop globally competitive technologies, know how, goods and services, has for a long time restricted West Indian influence in world affairs. This scenario is only beginning to change today.

D- The Political Economy of the West Indies from 1500 to 1950.

The civilization encountered by Christopher Columbus all but disappeared under the relentless onslaught of the Europeans. It was replaced by a strict political hierarchy of autocratic rule and large plantation economies of scale using armies of slaves to work the land. The Spaniards and Portuguese came first. They were followed by the French, the Dutch and English and finally by the Danes. The Portuguese were soon elbowed out and left with what is now Brazil and the Danes arrived late in the 1800's and became rooted in the present day U.S. Virgin Islands.

By 1550, many native populations in the West Indies had been decimated and were rapidly replaced by slaves from Africa. By 1600 they had ceased to be political and economic factors in the European mindset, although the last native population holdouts were not subdued militarily until almost 1800.

Colonization was a process of establishing systems of absolute rule under the principle of the divine right of kings. Only in the England's West Indian colonies, especially in those of the eastern Caribbean, did the rudiments of representative government emerge. While this embryonic democratization process was welcome, it was probably due less to altruism by the monarchs of England than to their being forced by their parliaments into power sharing arrangements. But even there, slavery held sway until the 1830's.

In all the islands, a rigorous pecking order from the crown to the crown's local viceroy, to the European landed gentry, to European naval and land forces to the freemen, indentured servants and finally to the slaves at the bottom, worked to execute the political policies and economic programs of the home country.

Self-government and self-determination in the West Indies were processes that evolved from the 1800's to the 1900's when independence movements accelerated. American influence increased dramatically in the aftermath of the Spanish-American war of 1898. Spain lost the war and was replaced by the United States as the dominant power in the region with England's and France's influence being simultaneously peacefully eclipsed.

Puerto Rico's political system changed to reflect the American system of constitutional democracy, and eventually it became a "commonwealth" as part of the United States. With "Operation Bootstrap," going into action in the late 1940's and early 1950's, economic growth development programs to modernize and industrialize the island turned it into one of the West Indies' higher income states. The main point here is that Puerto Rico would have found it difficult if not impossible to achieve any noteworthy development without a lasting connection with a superior economic power.

The experience of the other Spanish speaking Indies was not so positive. Cuba and the Dominican Republic were allowed for the most part, with American support, to develop their own forms of government and hence the "strong man" rule that prevailed on and off during their existence as Spanish colonies thrived well into the twentieth century. In the Dominican Republic it lasted into the 1960's, and the move to constitutional democracy took another two decades to complete. In Cuba, the despotism of Spain was replaced by the despotism of dictators that followed until the country was taken over by Fidel Castro and his communist followers in 1959. And here, a single party dictatorship committed to central economic planning has been in place to this day. Jamaica has been a constitutional democracy since the late 1950's when it became independent. However, the support that jumpstarted the Puerto Rican economy never reached Jamaica to the same extent, and the country remains relatively poor.

The political and economic history of the French speaking Indies has also been mixed. Haiti has been independent since the early 1800's but its dallies with democracy have fared poorly, and its economy has lagged far behind those of all other countries in the West Indies and the Western Hemisphere. The operating environment was different in the other former West Indian lands colonized by France. Guadeloupe, Martinique and the French side of St. Martin were granted self-government and incorporated into the French political system after 1945 as overseas departments. However, much of their development was and continues to be sponsored by metropolitan France.

French Guiana has not prospered to the same extent. This is because it was a penal colony until well into the twentieth century when the prison closed. It is of France's overseas departments and the French government is today investing heavily in its economy.

The record for the English speaking West Indies is also mixed, despite the fact that they have all developed into constitutional democracies. The most economically advanced state is Bermuda, its success due to its relationships with the United States and England. Lagging slightly behind are the Cayman Islands, the Bahamas and the Turks and Caicos whose successes may also be for the same reason. Heavy and ongoing transfusions of investment capital to feed the tourism and financial services industries have worked miracles to make those islands prosper.

Trinidad and Tobago has also prospered as a constitutional democracy since becoming independent in 1962. Its economic success is greatly due to a high-demand resource base (petroleum products) and economic policies its government has pursued that have helped it become less dependent on the largesse of North America and Europe.

The story is somewhat different with Jamaica (discussed above) and with the rest of the English speaking Indies who also became independent in the late 1950's and early 1960's. They are constitutional democracies but have not developed as rapidly as their wealthier neighbors. Many of them have struggled over the years with economic reverses and political instability.

The Dutch West Indies have generally fared better. Working democracies and fully self-governing, they are more closely linked to the economy of the Netherlands from which they draw financial support whenever necessary. It has also helped that St. Marten (the Dutch side) and the ABC islands (Aruba, Bonaire and Curacao) have been successful in positioning themselves as tourist destinations

8

Anguilla

I- Background

Anguilla is one of the smaller self-governing islands in the West Indies and represents in a microcosm what is both right and wrong about the West Indies. Situated at the northern end of the Leeward Islands between the Caribbean and the Atlantic, it is small, about 16 miles sixteen miles long and three miles wide at its longest and widest points, covering less than 48 square miles of land area. It is flat, the highest point being about 215 feet above sea level and water scarcity is a long term issue. Its saline ponds are a valuable resource from which salt can be commercially extracted but those alone are not enough to generate the level of economic activity it craves. It has therefore become highly dependent on the high-end tourist industry.

Six smaller islands belong to the tiny country: Dog Island, Prickly Pear Cays, Scrub Island, Sombrero (Hat) Island and Sandy Island. If those cays are included, the country's size increases to maybe 60 square miles, Anguilla and its outlying cays together are smaller than Martha's Vineyard and slightly bigger than Nantucket Island. [1]

The island group has a small permanent, all year-around population of between 13,000 and 15,000 people with a labor force engaged in commercial fishing, the salt industry and high-end boutique tourism industry in which most workers are employed. The main town, capital and seat of government is The Valley, less than five miles from Wallblake Airport. [2]

It is thought that French explorers passed by the island in 1556, believing it was eel shaped, "une anguille" it was called in French. The name became "Anguilla" in Spanish and remained unchanged when the English took over the island in 1650. It has been under British control ever since. Most of the people are of African descent although there is an admixture of Irish, descendants of indentured laborers who were imported by the English in the 1700's. The official language is English and most people are Protestant. Anglican, Baptist, Church of God, Jehovah's Witnesses and Seventh Day Adventist churches dot the landscape. There is also a small, active Roman Catholic population. [3]

From the 1960's until the 1980's, Anguilla was an "escape" for the "knowledgeable" tourist seeking a temporary laid-back hide-away from the pressures of every-day life. And sure enough, Anguilla did deliver the promise of that proverbial desert island with the white sandy beaches and palm trees with the picture perfect sunrises and sunsets. Sun baked and windswept beaches guaranteed golden tans without breaking a sweat, and cooling breezes at night turned the most modest dwellings into luxury sleeping accommodations at more than affordable prices. But the local inhabitants were not well off since most of the economic enterprises were subsistence in nature (fishing and housekeeping), labor-intensive and paid low-wages.

And so, Anguilla re-invented itself with the help of foreign investors who seized on the opportunity to turn the island into a tourist destination for very high-income vacationers.

Within two decades the island was transformed into a trendy and relatively expensive destination for celebrities, the super-rich, and tourists chasing that "once-in-a-lifetime" vacation experience. Anguilla's landscape is today dotted with dozens of up-scale resorts, villas and condominiums and any number of less expensive inns, more than eighty dining places and of course miles of open beaches and good shopping.

So then, is there a problem? The trouble is that high-end tourism in a small, out-of-the-way and hard-to-reach island may have limited long-term attraction. Small specialty resorts in remote places are not routinely repeat destinations for average vacation, business and convention travelers, the type of mass tourism that significantly creates value-added jobs and continuing income to a society. Because of its limited size, it is difficult for Anguilla to reach satisfactory economies of scale with selective high-profile tourism.

Further, tourism in the West Indies, with few exceptions, is subject to a seasonal index. Travel is more frequent during North America and Europe's cold weather months than during the heat of summer. A key to achieving competitive maximum economies of scale in the tourism industry is for a resort to position itself as a mass market and all-season destination like Disney World, Las Vegas or Aruba (sometimes dubbed the Las Vegas of the Caribbean). It should be noted in this context that the Disney brand has recognition globally and Las Vegas has casino-hotel tourism. However, Anguilla is a casino-free island, in keeping with its religiously conservative background.

Traveling to and from Anguilla is a challenge for the average vacationer. No non-stop commercial flights from North America or Europe land at Wallblake Airport, although it can accommodate private jets and smaller commercial craft. Direct flights are available from Sam Juan, Puerto Rico, and there are daily "puddle jumpers," air taxis and water taxis from neighboring islands. However, should large jets ever be available on a regular schedule, Anguilla's hotel facilities would be sorely strained.

It cannot be denied that upscale tourism has changed Anguilla for the better and that it has enhanced the local economy to a certain extent. The question is by how much? The island's current per capita GDP is $8,800 and average longevity is almost 80 years. By comparison, the current per capita GDP for Aruba is $22,000 and average longevity is also 80 years. [4]

Can it therefore be suggested that the Anguillan government should change course to move island's growth and development forward? The answer lies not in finding the right economic strategy; it lies instead in finding the right geo-political organization. The fact is that, as a basically self-governing country trying to capitalize on its limited resource base (small land size, small population and few resources (fish, salt and sun), it is too small. It would be much better off if it was united, as it once was, in a larger regional association, a subject that will be discussed in subsequent sections.

II- History

It was stated in Section A above that the French seemed to have been the first to sight the island in 1556, but it is probable that the Spanish preceded them by a few years. In any case it was not uninhabited, having already been settled for generations by the Carib Indians. The Caribs were run out by the French who were run out by the English in 1650, and settlers from St. Kitts established a small outpost. It is also believed that some of these early colonists came from Antigua and Barbados. Whatever their point of origin, they were English speaking and brought African slaves with them. The slaves do not appear to have been brought directly from Africa but were already in place elsewhere in the eastern Caribbean. [5]

Slaves from Senegal worked the fields in St. Kitts since the late 1500's, and a fortified enclosure was built on Nevis a few years later to serve as a depot and transfer point for the distribution of slaves throughout the Leeward Islands. The depot operated at capacity until well into the 1700's. By that time, over 100 slaves lived in Anguilla. When slavery was abolished as a legal institution by Great Britain in 1836, slaves of African descent were a majority of the population. Soon after slavery was ended, the English moved to slowly move their West Indian colonies in the direction of self-rule, especially after the economic benefits of maintaining those small communities became uncertain.

The reality was that the island fared poorly; it was too arid; the soil was too poor; there was little potable water, and the population never grew. The bottom line was that by the 1900's, Anguilla was becoming a financial drain on England as were some of its other colonies in the West Indies. It was paying for the island's upkeep and was receiving little revenue or very little of anything else in return. [6]

Unwilling to continue directly administering a colony whose population had shrunk to less than five thousand residents, England proposed in the early 1960's that Anguilla be merged into the proposed the formation of the Associated States of Kitts-Nevis-Anguilla. This new "nation" was to be internally self-governing but with the United .Kingdom, maintaining full control over its defense and foreign affairs.

Long story short, the idea was poorly received by Anguilla and the island rebelled in 1967, again in 1969, and the island became a British overseas territory in 1980 without any connection to St. Kitts-Nevis. It has retained that status ever since. [7]

III- Political Environments

Officially, Anguilla is a British Crown colony with discretionary internal self-governing rights. This is the same status enjoyed by the British Virgin Islands, the Cayman Islands and the Turks and Caicos. However, Anguilla and these other states are also classified as "non-self-governing territories by the United Nations Committee on Decolonization.

Anguilla has nevertheless been governed under a written charter called the Anguilla Constitutional Order since 1982 which was amended once in 1990. Under the current arrangement, the head of state is a royal governor Andrew N. George, who represents the English crown and is appointed by the Queen of England upon the advice of her ministers. The head of government is a chief minister, Osbourne Fleming, who is drawn from the dominant political party or coalition of parties, and has been in office since the year 2000.

The country has several political parties: The People's Progressive Party, the Anguilla United Party, the Anguilla National Alliance and the Anguilla Democratic Party. The National Alliance and the Democratic Party banded together with the Anguilla United Front to support Osbourne Fleming who won the Chief Minister's post in March, 2000. [8]

The island's political system and overall political climate is stable, and that is one of the reasons it has attracted outside investments in the tourist industry. This sudden surge in business activity has altered the country's social and demographic composition as well and may impact its future political organization.

The 2008 estimate indicates that most of Anguilla's permanent residents (90%) are the descendents of slaves of African ancestry. Minorities include Whites (5%) and those of mixed race (5%). This represents a change from the 1990's 2000 when 95% of the total population was classified as Black.

This increased diversity becomes even more obvious when the impact of immigration on the population mix and on its religious composition is considered. Today, 25% of the population is non-Anguillan (first generation arrivals or second generation offspring), most having come from the United States, the United Kingdom, the Dominican Republic and Jamaica. In addition, large numbers of Chinese, Mexican and South Asian workers have come to Anguilla since 2006 to ease labor shortages in the tourism industry.

In 1990, 41% of all Anguillan residents were classified as Anglican and another 33% were Methodist. This has now changed to 25% and 23% respectively. This is a reflection of the country's changing demographic composition as immigration continues to grow. [9]

The increased immigration and its impact on Anguillan society has been beneficial so far from the point of view that is has offset labor scarcities resulting from rapid growth in the tourist industry and has contributed to the country's recent fast economic growth. It is also inevitable that Anguilla's changing demographics and growing minorities are bound the change its political landscape in the near future..

IV- Economic Environments

Anguilla has three industries: fishing, tourism and retailing. Fishing is labor-intensive and exists to provide sustenance for the average family and for the many restaurants and resort establishments and probably contributes less than 20% to the country's GDP. The tourist industry contributes about 60% of GDP, and retailing (an offshoot of tourism) adds another 10%. The balance comes from government, banking and other miscellaneous services. About 7,000 people participate in the labor force, most working in the hotel industry and government service sector. The poverty rate is 20%.

Anguilla has no currency of its own, although the US Dollar and English Pound Sterling is widely accepted. It uses the East Caribbean dollar, as do many other countries in the eastern Caribbean. The ECC dollar or XCD, its currency code, has been stable at ECC 2.7 per US $ since 1976 when it was first fixed (pegged) to the American dollar.

The closest that the country has to a central bank is the National Bank of Anguilla or NBA. It came into existence in 1984 as an offshoot of the Bank of America National Trust and Savings Association. Its main function is to serve as a retail bank, although it has investments in insurance companies, credit card processing firms and offers financing for corporate customers and public sector projects. Due to the current global financial crisis that has also impacted Anguilla, its future is uncertain.

An attempt was made in the 1990's to develop a financial services industry that offered foreign clients tax haven programs. Investment banks opened facilities in The Valley but the industry never developed to the extent that it did elsewhere (the Cayman Islands for example). A major obstacle was the growing aggressiveness of governments in Europe and North America in trying to control the activities of tax havens.

It is estimated that Anguilla hosts up to 200,000 tourists each year. Half of these are day trippers (tourists visiting neighboring islands and flying and/or ferrying over for a day of sightseeing, shopping and sunbathing. Water, energy, labor and land shortages prevent the continued rapid growth of the tourism industry. [10]

There is, however, a deeper problem, even if a way is found to expand the industry. The country has an annual recorded per capita GDP of only $8,800 despite its vibrant economy with a total population of 14,000 residents. This compares poorly with Aruba's 112,000 residents whose economy generates an annual per capita income of $22,000. It is possible that Anguilla's overall income is somewhat understated.

Now, according to the CIA World Fact Book, Anguilla has more recently been identified as a "transshipment point for South American narcotics destined for the US and Europe." The drug trade might therefore account for the discrepancy. [11]

It would seem from the above data, assuming it is correct, that it does not ring true. The country features more than twenty resort hotels (albeit a relatively small number of rooms and sleeping accommodations), seventy eateries of different price categories and numbers of souvenir, wearing apparel, jewelry and sundries shops. It is difficult to imagine that all this hustle and bustle can only muster $8,800 per capita including reasonable return rates to investors. The per capita income or product data also does not take into consideration the distribution of income situation. If perfect income distribution existed, it would mean that Anguilla's society was economically egalitarian. This is probably not quite so since some individuals and families on the island enjoy living standards higher than do most of the people.

Several explanations are possible:

1- The official data is incorrect and does not reflect real conditions in Anguilla.

2- The economy is not doing as well as it is being touted. If that is the case, then the concept of tourism investment as a means of triggering growth and development may be misplaced and that Anguilla's tourism industry may not have enough potential to pay its workers an adequate wage and raise living standards significantly.

3- There exists an underground economy in which income is being unreported and is therefore not being recorded. This means income is being siphoned off by investors and other key players in the economy with the added possibility that it is being drawn out of the country for investment or spending elsewhere.

The question that should be raised at this point is whether Anguilla's diminutive size and tiny population are able to achieve any appreciable economies of scale in any sort of enterprise that could significantly raise living in a twenty first century post industrial setting without being part of a greater and broader political association.

V- International Affairs

Because of its status as an overseas territory of the United Kingdom, Anguilla does not field embassies or consulates in other countries. It is an associate member of CARICOM, the Caribbean Community, formerly called the Caribbean Common Market, but has no voting rights. Most of its international affairs and relations tend to be of a commercial nature and they are mostly with North America and Europe. As a dependency, it is not recognized as an independent nation and is hence not a member of the United Nations or any other international governing organization.

VI- SWOT Analysis

1- Strengths

Small country size, small population and a poor resource base but balmy weather are strengths in the sense that the island is not a threat to anyone and offers a welcome mat to everyone.

2- Weaknesses

Those same strengths are weaknesses conspiring against the country's capacity to develop large economy of scale industries that can quickly raise incomes from wages and salaries. The small scale tourism industry in Anguilla could succeed in this respect, but only if its workers can become the highest paid housekeepers, bellhops and waiters in the world.

3- Opportunities

An alternative approach, using the education, experience and know-how of the labor force as an opportunity, could be to supplement the tourism industry with high-value, high paying outsource activities that help multinational companies service their larger markets. The investments required might need to be of a longer term nature, but the real returns to investors and workers might be much greater.

4- Threats

Hurricanes are the only physical threats that could disrupt Anguilla's tourism industry. In recent years, violent storms have struck neighboring islands, leaving them in shambles and their economies reeling. Anguilla has been lucky and spared, but it hard to predict the effect a hurricane would have on Anguilla if it were to take a direct hit.

VII- Summary and conclusions

Anguilla's background is typical of many of the countries and territories in the West Indies. It bears the scars of a society based on slave labor and its history reveals that for the last two centuries it has struggled not to become one of civilizations economic back-waters. It is today not a rich country; nor is it poor. The tourism industry has had positive effects on improving the country's economy, but it has not made it rich and it has not yet addressed its long term growth and development. It has not resolved of problems of 20% of the population who live below the poverty line, unless those who are labeled as living in poverty have un-reportable income sources. The country is much too small and much too dependent on the outside world to unilaterally shape its own destiny and is therefore unable to add its weight to shaping major decisions in the world.

It is fascinating to speculate what would happen if Anguilla was to come upon untold riches of gold, crude oil and other scarce resources in vital demand by the rest of the world. In all probability it would overnight be annexed as a suburb of London or New York, and that in the final analysis might be in the best interest of Anguilla's people.

Anguilla

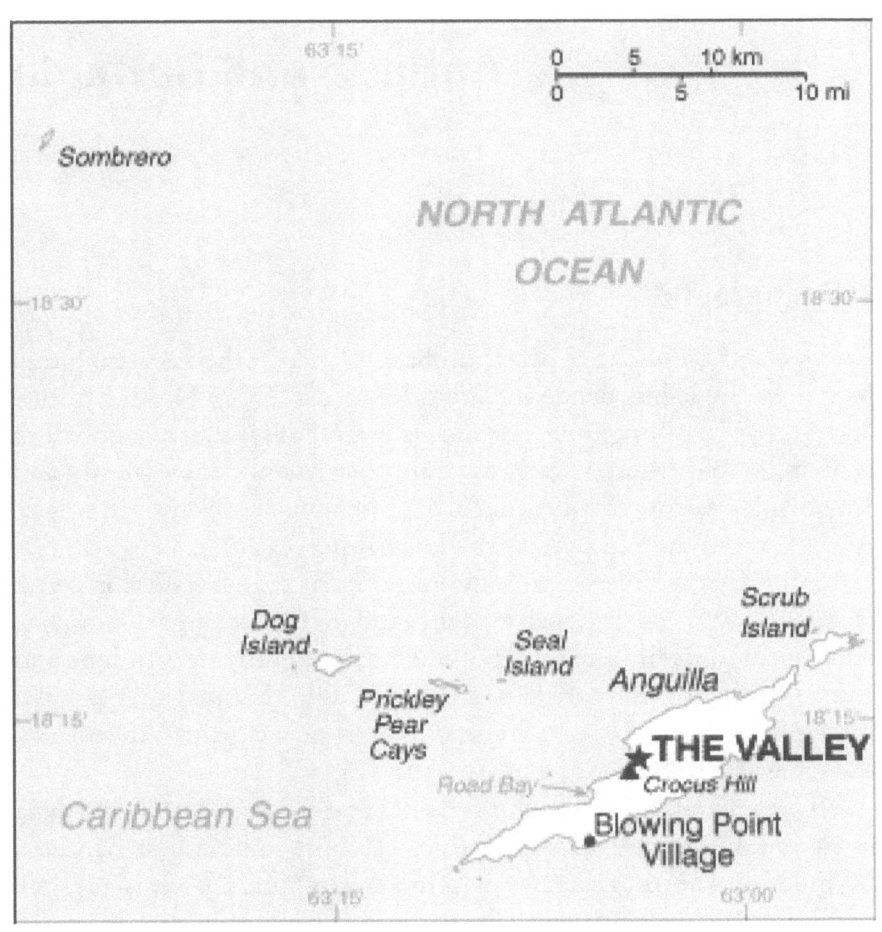

Source: CIA World Fact Book, October 2008 (cia.org/library).

9

Antigua and Barbuda

I- Background

Antigua and Barbuda are two Caribbean islands in the Leeward group forming a single independent nation. Located at 17.03 North Latitude and 61.48 West Longitude, Barbuda is Anguilla's smaller neighbor and is 35 miles to the north-northeast. Saint Barthelemy, Saint Martin and Anguilla lay northwest of Antigua. Their names are Spanish in origin, Antigua meaning "old" and Barbuda meaning "bearded." [1]

Saint Kitts and Nevis and Saint Eustatius lay to the west. Montserrat is the southwest. To the south are the islands of Guadeloupe, Dominica, and Martinique, the remainder of the Leeward group. Martinique and Saint Lucia (the most northern of the Windward Islands) are separated by the Saint Lucia Passage. South of Saint Lucia is Saint Vincent and the Grenadines, Barbados and Grenada. [2]

If comparative geographical benchmarks are helpful, Antigua is 14 miles long and 11 miles wide, or 154 square miles. Barbuda, 30 miles due north, is smaller with 68 square miles. Both islands are smaller than Catalina Island off the coast of California, at 176 square miles, Nantucket Island off Cape Cod at 105 square miles and Martha's Vineyard at 87 square miles. Antigua and Barbuda's combined population in 2008 is estimated at 85,000 with most of the people living on the island of Antigua. [3]

The country's topography is different from that of Anguilla. Barbuda is fairly flat and Antigua also has an extensive lowland coastal perimeter of limestone and coral, but much of its interior is quite hilly and its higher ranges are volcanic in nature. The highest point on Antigua is Boggy Peak (1319 ft) but the island has not suffered any volcanic activity in its recent history. Like in many Caribbean islands, arable land is in short supply. Its supply is limited to 19% of its land area, severely restricting the cultivation of permanent crops.

Antigua has a deeply indented shoreline with natural harbors and many beaches that have made the island a magnet for tourists and the sailing fraternity, especially during the winter months. The capital city, St. John's, with a steady population in its metropolitan area of 30,000, boasts a deep water port that can accommodate the largest cruise ships. Barbuda's surrounding waters tend to be shallow, but it has a small harbor on its western side. [4]

Despite the published facts that over 90% of the population is of African descent and another 5% is Caucasian with the balance being classified as other, Antiguan society in reality can best be described as being pluralistic and of mixed race and ethnicity. Many of its current residents have originated in any number of other countries from many parts of the world.

It is interesting to note that the more recent Caucasian arrivals are from Canada and the United States. Indeed, there is said that the American ex-patriot community, numbering roughly 4,500 residents, in Antigua is the largest in the English West Indies in the eastern Caribbean. There are also Caucasians of English, Irish, Portuguese and Spanish descent. In addition, the country is home to small communities of Sephardic Jews and Levantine Arabs from Lebanon, Palestine and Syria. [5]

The country's religious mix is worthy of note. Protestants predominate at 75% of the total population with half of them being Anglicans, the rest being Methodists, Moravians, Pentecostals and Seventh-Day Adventists. Another 15% of the people are Catholic, and 10% are Rastafarians, Moslems, Sephardic Jews and members of other religious groups.[6]

Another interesting feature of Antiguan society is immigration. People from Asia and elsewhere in the Caribbean (the Dominican Republic is a major point of origin in recent years) have gravitated to Antigua to seek employment in the growing tourism industry and other related service sector enterprises. The assimilation of off-shore minorities has to date gone smoothly.

The country's per capita GDP is $18,500. Life expectancy at birth is presently 73 years and the literacy rate is over 90%. The country decided in 1998 to become a health and medical care center for the Caribbean and is working to complete the Mt. Saint John Medical Center, a state-of-the-art hospital. It also has two medical schools, a government operated college, an institute specializing in information technology and a campus that is part of the University of West Indies. The availability of internet based on-line services also makes it possible for increasing numbers of Antiguan residents to pursue on-line degrees. [8]

II- History [9]

It is said that the first inhabitants of Antigua and Barbuda probably island-hopped their way from the American mainland about 4400 years ago. They were apparently edged out much later by the Arawak Indians who were in turn forced to relocate by the Caribs who were finally decimated by the Europeans. Called Waddali by the Caribs, some locals still call Antigua "the land of Wadadli."

It was during Christopher Columbus's second trip in 1493 that Antigua was discovered and named Santa Maria de la Antigua in honor of a church in Seville, Spain. Antigua and Barbuda were settled initially by the Spanish who quickly lost interest when they found little evidence of gold or any other mineral wealth. The English replaced the Spanish in 1632 and, except for a brief period of French occupation in 1666, the two islands stayed under British rule until independence in the twentieth century. The islands were formally joined into the British Empire in the Acts of Union of 1707. The Acts of Union actually concerned the impending union of Scotland and England by their respective monarchs and parliaments and had little to do with England's off-shore colonies. However, those treaties, in addition to linking Scotland to England as part of a single political union, gave England the opportunity to lock in its colonies as part of a broader "empire" controlled by the government in London.

Several "acts" passed by the English parliament pursuant to the original Acts of Union over the next century and a half eventually led to the creation of the Commonwealth of Nations. Its original purpose was to serve as an umbrella organization for all of England's colonies as they moved toward self- government.

Independence for Antigua and Barbuda with Commonwealth status came in 1981. It is interesting to note that the country is officially known as the Monarchy of Antigua and Barbuda with Queen Elizabeth II as its Sovereign and head of state as represented on site by a governor-general. Slavery had existed in the islands since the early 1500's, but it reached its full flower under the English for their sugar plantations. The abolishment of slavery occurred in 1834 by an act of Parliament whose timing coincided with the decline of the sugar plantation system in the islands, a trend leading to a long period of economic stagnation.

III- Political Environments [10]

The country's contemporary political history begins with the ascendancy of the Bird family to power in the early 1900's. Sir Vere Cornwall Bird was born in the capital city of St. John's in 1910 and died in 1999. Except for primary school attendance, he had no formal education. He worked for the Salvation Army and early in his life he immersed himself in politics through the local trade union movement. He was a union activist and rose in the ranks to become the president of Antigua Trades and Labor Union in 1943.

With the union as his source of support, he was elected to the colonial legislature in 1945 and used his new position to form the Antigua Labor Party. He was the party leader until 1994 when age and poor health finally forced him into retirement. As head of the ALP, he became the country's first and only chief minister, the first and last premier and the first prime minister from 1984 to 1994. Antigua's international airport was named VC Bird International Airport in 1985.

Throughout much of Vere Bird's tenure, Antigua was governed as family enterprise in close cooperation with the ALP. When Vere Bird retired in 1994, he was succeeded in power by his son, Lester Bryant Bird.

Born in New York City in 1938, Lester Bird was brought up in his father's image to eventually assume the helm of government, but he was successful in his own right and increased the power and wealth of the Bird family. He served as chairman of the ALP from 1971 to 1994 when he gave up the office to assume the job of prime minister, a position he held until 2004 when the ALP was finally defeated in open election by the United Progressive Party (UPP).

Much has been written about the alleged despotism of the Bird era, and certainly the country has endured its share of the cronyism and corruption that often accompanies governments where power is concentrated in the hands of a single family and its clique of close associates. However, it must also be stressed that the constitutional democracy that was envisioned by England as it gradually sought to divest itself of direct control over its West Indian colonies probably had to proceed in stages. It was necessary for England to make sure in the closing years of World War II that its overseas territories were to be left in a stable state and in a position to govern themselves from the outset. In Antigua and Barbuda, leaving the new government temporarily in the hands of a few individuals and families enjoying popular backing seems to have had long term benefits. If nothing else, V. C. Bird must be given the credit for having led the country from colonialism to full independence.

Antigua today is a constitutional democracy based on a federal parliamentary system. The head of state is the British monarchy represented by an appointed governor-general. The governor-general selected by the Crown in 2007 was Louise-Lake Tack, the first female to hold that post in Antigua. Dame Louise-Lake Tack is Antiguan born and spent a good part of her life in the practice of law and as an appeals judge in the Antigua justice system before being tapped for her current position. [11]

The prime minister, Baldwin Spencer (the leader of the United Progressive party), is the head of government. The parliament is bicameral with a Senate (17 members appointed by the governor-general) and a House of Representatives (17 members elected on a "first past the post" (plurality) basis. The last elections in 2004 routed the ALP, leaving it with only four of seventeen seats, A new election is scheduled for 2009, and it is expected that the party may make a comeback. [12]

Issues of current importance facing Antigua's government are focused on the growing problems of water management and developing new water resources, diversifying and expanding the country's agricultural base, non-tourism services development, industrial growth and trying to increase income from the increasing number of cruise ships stopping at Saint Johns. The problem here, as it is elsewhere, is that tourists making the rounds of the West Indies on cruise ships spend most of their money on board and contribute little to the local economy. Further, very little cruise ship income from passenger fares is ever returned to local ports-of-call.

IV- Economic Environments

The characteristic typical of Antigua and Barbuda and of most of the West Indies is the scarcity of useable and/or marketable natural resources. Even water and arable land are scarce. This has worked to the long term disadvantage of the Indies once its position as a major sugar producing area and transit point for the slave trade catering to the labor needs of the early United States was usurped by changing economic times and the anti-slavery movement.

The traditional economy of Antigua and Barbuda, based on plantation (sugar and some cotton) and subsistence agriculture (vegetables and pineapples –also produced for export as well as for the local market), continued after the abolition of slavery in 1834 until well into the 1950's. It was complemented by fishing and livestock for local consumption and finally to meet tourism demand. [13]

Visitors were few and far between until jet transportation in the late 1950's made travel on direct commercial flights feasible, practical and relatively inexpensive. Until then, a trip to Antigua and other East Caribbean islands involved taking a long, expensive and tedious journey with a stop-over in Puerto Rico. The first passenger jets began non-stop flights to Puerto Rico in 1960. The flights took about four hours. A transfer on a regional airline took another two to four hours, depending on the number of stops along the way. By that time several high-profile resort hotels had opened along with banks that offered tax-sheltering services. It cannot be denied that the dawn of the jet age made fast, long distance travel possible and distant islands accessible opened the floodgates of Caribbean tourism. The Antiguan government took note of these developments and made promoting tourism and financial services cornerstones of economic planning.

By the mid-1960's, word of Antigua's dry, pleasant weather made its way to major tourist markets, turning it into a regular, repeat winter vacation destination for intrepid families chasing peace, quiet and the sun. Almost overnight, the trickle of vacationers became a torrent, spurring a construction boom in resort hotels. This also increased employment in all industries connected with supporting the tourist trade and, later, financial services.

However, it was not until the 1990's and the present decade that the tourism industry rapidly morphed into its current state. Certainly, the scheduling of non-stop flights from major markets along the eastern seaboard of the United States and the construction of new full service, all-inclusive resort hotels were responsible for the upsurge in tourist traffic. The growth of the financial services industry as investment banks took root in the country, making it a destination for seekers of tax shelters, was also a factor that placed Antigua on the global economic map.

One cannot ignore the importance of tourism and financial services to Antigua. It transformed an economically marginalized country into a progressive and competitive society. In 2006, the last year for which data was available for this printing, Antigua and Barbuda hosted 265,000 visitors who sojourned one night or longer. [14]

Many thousands more were day-trippers from visiting cruise ships, but the amount of income they contributed to the economy was limited to their expenditure on souvenirs.

Recorded tourism receipts for 2006 were $327 million, or, $1,234.00 per visitor. Given a population of 70,000, this amounted to a per capita GDP for that year of $4,671.00, or 43% of Antigua's total per capita GDP of $11,000.

A downside of this type of mass all-inclusive, full service tourism has been the relative decline of the middle and high-end restaurant trade. Many eateries dot the islands of Antigua and Barbuda and most of them cater to the local population. Tourists generally dine at their hotels or on cruise ships where food is included in the passenger fare.

If, according to the U.S. Department of Commerce, tourism and financial services contribute a full 77% of Gross Domestic Product and tourism alone adds up to 43%, then by extrapolation, financial services yields another 34%. Agriculture contributes a mere 3.0%, and manufacturing activities (alcohol, textiles and construction) add another 20%. No reliable data on the ratio of the population below the poverty line was found at this time. [15]

Despite the pre-eminent role of tourism and financial services in moving Antigua's economy forward, annual per capita GDP is low when compared to that of high income nations. This raises the question, as in the case of Anguilla, of whether the role of tourism and financial services is under-stated or whether revenues are misappropriated and/or siphoned off by vested interests. To this day, the country remains import dependent and dependent on tourism to sustain its economy.

Crime has become a problem and the financial services industry has fallen under local and international scrutiny for allegedly supporting tax evaders from the United States and Europe. In addition, it is considered a major transshipment point for narcotics bound for the US and Europe.

Antigua and Barbuda uses the Eastern Caribbean Dollar (EC$) which is pegged to the U.S. dollar at EC$2.7 = U.S.$1.00. The peg is stable and means that that the EC$ rises and falls against currencies not pegged to the U.S. dollar. The practical implication of this peg is that the cost of importing for Antiguans rises as the U.S. dollar falls against the Euro and other key currencies.

V- International Affairs

The country maintains diplomatic relations with the United States and most countries in the world including the People's Republic of China. It is a member of the United Nations, the Commonwealth of Nations, the Caribbean Common Market (CARICOM), the CARICOM Single Market and Economy (CSME), the Eastern Caribbean Regional Security System (RSS), the Organization of American States and the Organization of Eastern Caribbean States

Antigua and Barbuda is an activist country in its international relations, often taking positions that work against the interests of the United States. However, it has worked hard with Washington to maintain basically friendly relations. The result has been that the U.S. has given and continues provide the country with considerable financial and economic support through the United States Agency for International Development, the Caribbean Basin Initiative, the World Bank and the Caribbean Development Bank.

Because of its strategic location in the Leeward Islands near maritime shipping lanes, Antigua has long been of importance to American national security and has accepted an on-going U.S. naval presence. The naval base was turned over to Antigua in 1995 and today serves as a Coast Guard training center. Antigua and the United States are also signatories to a number of mutual defense, legal assistance and extradition treaties.

VI- SWOT Analysis

1- Strengths

The strength of Antigua and Barbuda is the attractive, balmy weather which is a natural magnet for international tourism. The population is generally well-educated and the labor force is disciplined and trained. Its friendly relationship with the United States is another strength from the point of view that the country can depend on Washington for continued economic, financial and political support.

2- Weaknesses

Antigua's major weaknesses mirror those of most eastern Caribbean islands. Its small size and population and its paucity of natural, marketable resources make it difficult for the country to move forward without significant inputs from high income countries. In addition, Antigua's weather, with which it is blessed, is also a curse. The islands are in a hurricane zone, and ever so often, they are battered by storms that repeatedly tear at their infrastructure, making it difficult to maintain forward economic momentum.

3- Opportunities

Many investment opportunities outside of the tourism and financial services industries exist. It has been suggested that the hotel industry be expand into casinos, an approach taken by Aruba. However, considerable opposition to the concept exists in Antigua on religious grounds. Further, casino gambling creates its own host of problems. A more practical investment opportunity, taking advantage of the country's educated population, lies in the information technology industries. This is a path taken by Barbados which has established itself as an offshore information processing center.

4- Threats

Antigua is not faced with any current external threats. The country's leadership is well received in the international corridors of power and is not involved in local or external disputes that threaten to destabilize the operating order of its society.

VII- Summary and conclusions

Antigua's response to its vulnerability to the caprices of its climate, its limited resource base, to dependence on tourism and financial services and its exposure to severe external economic shocks, has been to encourage growth in communications and more recently on internet gambling. These have been and continue to be the usual parochial approaches to economic growth and development in many areas.

The question to be asked, in terms of helping Antigua close the gap between its income and that of wealthier trading and investment partners like the United States, is the type of economic endeavors it should concentrate on. The question is valid if one assumes that the current level of output generated in Antigua has been correctly reported and that its society enjoys a more-or-less equal distribution of income. The question is invalid if the real level of economic activity is under-reported or if it is misappropriated. This had been the fear during the Bird years. The hope is that political reform since 2004 has improved the country's prospects to accelerate its development.

Antigua and Barbuda

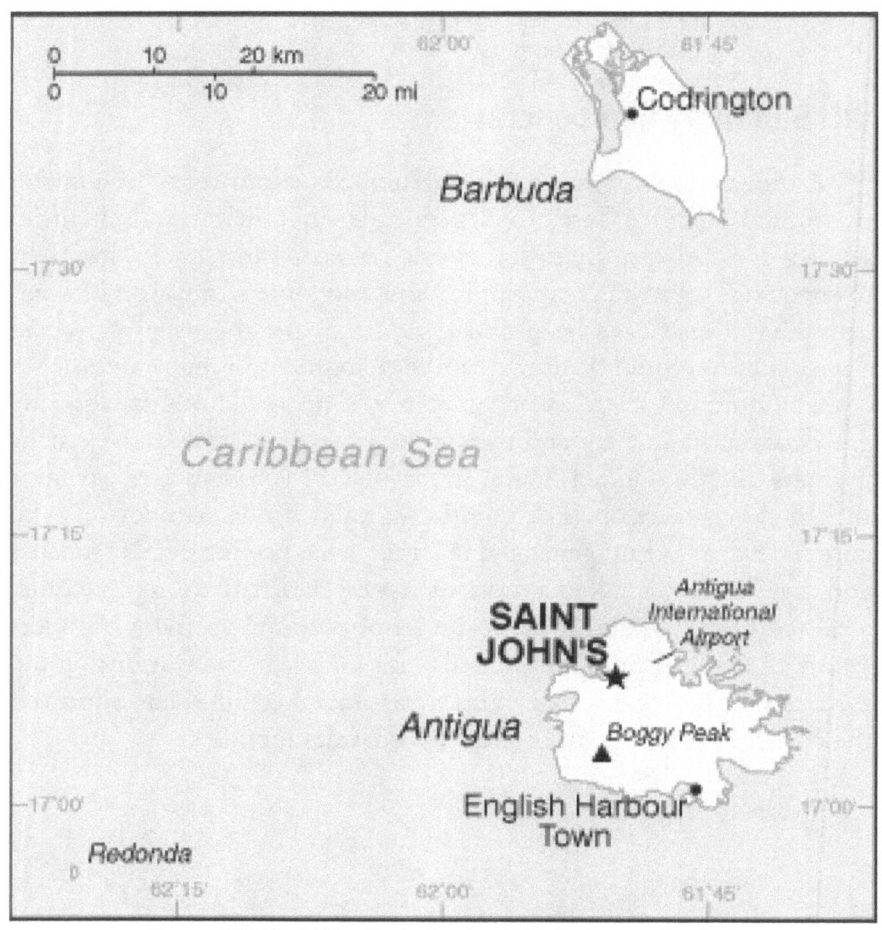

Source: CIA World Fact Book, October 2008 (web accessed 10/08)

10

Barbados

I- Background

The country of Barbados is technically an island in the Atlantic Ocean and is not part of the Eastern Caribbean that forms part of the Caribbean basin. It is at the apex of a triangle between St. Lucia to the north and St. Vincent to the south about 100 miles east of the two islands. [1] Hence, it is classified as one of the Windward Islands despite the fact that it differs geographically and geologically from the rest of the eastern Caribbean.

Most of its eastern Caribbean neighbors are the top-sides of a volcanic ridge extending in a convex arc from the Greater Antilles almost all the way down the Venezuelan coast. Barbados, in contrast, is the flattened top of a coral and limestone mountain that drops precipitously several miles to the bottom of the sea. [2]

It is larger than Antigua, [3] 21 miles in length and 14 miles wide, giving it a total land area of 294 square miles. (4) If comparisons are useful, it is only slightly smaller than New York City which occupies 304.8 square miles of land. (5). However, its population totals about 280,000 as opposed to over 8 million for New York City. [6]

The origins of the name "Barbados" are interesting and also in some dispute. As a pure linguistic expression it means "bearded one" in the Portuguese language of the 1400 and 1500's. The first Europeans to have seen and named the island are said to have been the Portuguese who were supposed to be on the way to Brazil. [7] Still, one can wonder why it would have been given such a name. It has been suggested that the name stood for the bearded fig tree, a type of banyan growth that can reach heights of 50 feet, projects aerial roots down from high branches and flourishes in the Caribbean, Florida, coastal Central America and the north coast of South America. It has also been argued that white froth from seas breaking against reefs surrounding Barbados may have been responsible for the name.

Barbados is basically flat, its highest elevation being Mount Hillaby which stands tall at 1,100 feet. The weather is tropical, but the land has generally been spared the ravages of hurricanes and is sufficiently fertile to support an extensive plantation economy. Tobacco was the staple until the early 1800's when it was replaced by sugarcane. Sugar and rum are still important to the economy but are today dwarfed by tourism, financial services and light industry. [8]

About half of the country's population lives in the parish of St. Michael, the county or province that includes Bridgetown, the capital city, in the country's southwestern sector. Ninety percent of all Barbadians are of African descent, sometimes refer to themselves as Afro-Bajans. Another 5% are Anglo-Bajans (English, Irish, Canadians or Americans) or Euro-Bajans (expatriates from the European mainland. [9]

Within that hyphenated Baja category are significant Chinese, Hindus (India), Moslems (India, Pakistan and Bangladesh) and Arab-Bajans who are of Christian Lebanese and Syrian descent and whose numbers are steadily growing. The last 5% of the population is mixed or Creole. At this point it should be noted that while the country's overall annual growth is low, about 0.03%, the growth of the non-black and non-white minorities is growing faster and their share of GDP is growing even faster. There has lately been an influx of immigration from the Republic of Guyana, but it is too early to tell how these new arrivals will impact the overall demographic situation. [10]

In any case, prosperity has not by-passed Barbados in recent years. Its average annual per capita GDP is about $17,297 and average longevity at birth is 76.6 years. [11]

The main economic pursuit until the middle of the past century was labor intensive agriculture in sugar cane production. This has changed to higher paid employment in services which today is the main source of economic output. According to the World Bank's published human development index (HDI), Barbados ranked 31st in the world in 2006 and has consistently ranked among the top fifty countries in the world. Indeed, it ranks 3rd in the Americas behind Canada and the United States. Barbados continued to rank 31st in the world in the 2007-2008 period with a score of 0.892 as opposed to Antigua and Barbuda that ranked 57th with a score of 0.815. [12]

It must of course be kept in mind that the United States ranks 12th with a score of 0.951 and longevity at birth of 77.9 years and an annual per capita GDP of $41,890 in 2006.

As in all the English speaking eastern Caribbean, Protestantism predominates with 67% of the population with most belonging to the Anglican Church. About 10% of Barbadians are Catholic; the rest being Jehovah's Witnesses, Hindus, Muslims and Jewish. [13]

II- History

Amerindians are said to have come from South America and settled Barbados several centuries before the birth of Christ. They were followed by the Arawak people who were followed by the Caribs who were also from South America. The Caribs decimated their predecessors and were the sole inhabitants of the island until the arrival of Portuguese in the early 1500's. The Portuguese may have enslaved the Caribs but no clear evidence to that effect exists. It is mainly conjecture, but the Carib Indians throughout the Caribbean were clever, aggressive and hardy fighters who were difficult to pacify and enslave. The more probable explanation for their eradication is that they succumbed to the epidemic diseases brought by Europeans, most likely tuberculosis and small pox. [14]

In any case, the Portuguese found little use for the land and left for South America by 1610. When the English arrived in 1625, they found Barbados largely abandoned. Until Barbados became independent in 1966, Barbados remained under continuous British rule, although the Anglo settlers enjoyed a good measure of local autonomy. The Barbadian parliament, the House of Assembly, a legislature proposed by Henry Powel, opened its doors for business and began passing laws in 1639. The Spanish, French and Dutch had little interest in contesting

England for the land because they were more interested in the larger Caribbean islands. [15]

From the outset, Barbados as a colony prospered but at the expense of becoming a slave state dominated by large plantations and their owners. The crop of choice until the early 1800's was tobacco. It was replaced by sugar cane introduced by Brazilian Jews and within a generation it dominated the Barbadian economy until well into the 1950's.

Slavery was a bloody and unhappy experience for Barbados. African Blacks brought over to work the plantations proved to be restive and the result was that the country's development from the mid 1600's to 1834 was marred by many slave rebellions that were violently suppressed with much loss of life. [16]

England abolished the slave trade throughout its possessions in 1807 did not abolish the institution of slavery until 1834. In the meantime, one of the major slave rebellions in the entire Caribbean, although it was far dwarfed by the successful uprising in Haiti in 1800, occurred in Barbados in 1816. Twenty thousand slaves from seventy plantations took up arms but were defeated after a considerable loss of life. [17]

Life changed little for the freed slaves after 1834. They still had to making a living, and most of them stayed on the plantations, toiling the fields under deplorable conditions that probably little better than during the era of legalized slavery. Indeed, it can be argued that in certain instances the freed slaves and their descendants may have been worse off since their former owners were no longer responsible for their upkeep and well being.

By 1850, Barbados was a major sugar producer and exporter, the bulk of its output going to Europe and North America. Chronic labor shortages were addressed through the use of convict labor and by mandating that all new immigrants had to sign a contract in which they agreed to do plantation work for five to seven years. Those who arrived with money were encouraged to invest in the sugar industry or to become planters themselves.

Barbadian sugar cane dominated the Caribbean sugar industry until it was confronted by other producers in the West Indies. In the English speaking West Indies, plantations in the Leeward Islands and Jamaica, with better technology and more advanced methods of cultivation, became to be formidable competitors. In time, however, even they had to come face to face with the greater competitive economies of scale that could be achieved by the larger producers in Cuba, the Dominican Republic, Haiti and Puerto Rico. The real problem emerged in the twentieth century however when countries like the United States and Brazil entered world markets with their own production. World sugar distribution and supply chains were further disrupted when the United States began imposing quotas on imported sugar that placed its foreign suppliers on an allocation system. [18]

Errol Walton Barrow, Barbados' first prime minister when it became independent in 1966, can be credited for peacefully planning and guiding the country's transition from a cheap labor agricultural colony to an advanced and globally competitive services and light manufacturing economy. [19]

III- Political Environments

Barbados has traveled a long, zigzag road to independence and its history shows that it did not always enjoy cordial relations with England and sought to cultivate a long term political connection with Canada. A group of wealthy and influential plantation owners in 1884 formed the Barbados Agricultural Society and communicated with the government of Canada with the goal of joining the Canadian Confederation. That effort led nowhere, mainly because most Barbadian farmers, who were White Anglos, felt safer under the British protective umbrella. Still, the movement for separation from England continued into the twentieth century. Most of the pro-separation sentiment came from the former slaves.

It gained momentum when descendants of emancipated slaves organized and formed the Barbados Progressive League in the 1930's that eventually became the Barbados Labor Party. But it was not until the late 1940's that power from the landed farmers was wrested away by newly politically enfranchised voters in open elections. The amazing aspect of the journey from a White Anglo dominated colony of England to the creation of a basically Black African democracy was that it proceeded largely without violence once slavery ended. Barbados joined the West Indies Federation in 1958 and was a founding member of the Caribbean Free Trade Association (CARIFTA) in 1964. It finally gained its independence in 1966 within the Commonwealth of Nations.

It is today a constitutional monarchy presiding over a parliamentary democracy. The head of state is the monarch of England, currently Queen Elizabeth II, who is represented in by a governor-general, a Barbadian national, as in the case of Antigua. [20]

The Barbadian government mirrors to a certain degree England's political organization. The Executive branch is the office of prime minister that functions in consultation with the governor-general. The prime minister forms a governing cabinet mainly from the majority party.

The legislative branch is a fifty-one seat bi-cameral parliament, a House of Assembly and a Senate. The House of Assembly has thirty representatives elected for five years by universal suffrage. The governor-general appoints the Senate's 21 members. Twelve are appointed the advice and consent of the prime minister, two with the advice and consent of the leader of the opposition party, and seven at the governor-general's discretion in an attempt to fairly represent the individual parishes of Barbados. [21]

Elections in 2008 resulted in David Thompson winning the prime minister's post in Barbados. It should be noted that policy differences between the two parties tend to be minor and that elections are won and lost on sometimes trivial personality issues. Order and stability seem to be the twin cornerstones of Barbadian political behavior.

The judiciary is independent and includes all lower courts established by law and a Supreme Court which comprises of a four judge High Court and a four judge Court of Appeals. The Chief Justice serves on both the high court and the court of appeals. The court of last resort is the Judicial Committee of the Crown's Privy Council in London. Decisions of the Privy Council are binding. [22]

The Barbadian judicial system has up to now been referring its appeals to the Privy Council in London. This is changing as the process of judicial review slowly transitions to the Caribbean Court of Justice (CCJ).

There is also speculation that Barbados may soon declare itself to be a republic. If and when that happens, the English Crown may need to be replaced by an elected president. What roles a president and prime minister may have in this new form of organization is still being discussed. [23]

A recent common complaint in many quarters has been that the government in power is not dealing as effectively as it could with public safety issues. Barbadians have also been expressing concerns about upward pressure on real estate prices resulting from increased foreign demand for land. These two domestic issues are bound to have an impact of the direction of government policies in the near future.

IV- Economic Environments

If a city's skyline is any indication of economic achievement, Barbados's capital and largest city, Bridgetown, is a small metropolis whose architecture mixes the old with the new. It is a shopping paradise for tourists and locals who crowd the streets with cell phones glued to their ears. Vehicle traffic is the usual nightmare of any city as cars and trucks snake their way through busy thoroughfares lined with office buildings, many of which harbor at ground level retail stores and restaurants of every variety, including a fair sprinkling of internationally known fast food eateries. Bridgetown is the picture of a city on the move and is a symbol of a country with a vibrant economy.

The original goal of the Barbadian government was to turn the country into the smallest developed country in the world by 2008. Government officials believe it may still happen by 2025. The Barbadian economy stagnated during the late 1990's and the first few years of the twenty-first century. It has recovered since 2004 and Gross Domestic Product has been experiencing an average annual growth rate of 3%. That growth is continuing in 2008. Tourism plays a major role in driving the country's growth, although most visitors are day trippers coming off cruise ships. About 570,000 tourists visited Barbados in 2006. This rose to over 600,000 in 2007. However, the majority of vacationers were cruise ship passengers who spent only a few hours ashore.

Barbados has nevertheless become a vacation destination for Americans, Canadians and Europeans. Two developments have helped plant the country on the tourist map. The first was a boom in hotel construction and renovation that began at the start of the decade to make more resort facilities available. The second was an increase in the number of direct and non-stop flights from North America and Europe. Barbados had also attracted many American, Canadian and European "second-homers" who live in the country permanently or during the winter months. It is estimated that 3,000 American expatriates permanently reside in Barbados today.

Being relatively prosperous and highly educated, the financial services sector, typical of many emerging markets and high income countries, is expanding rapidly as evidenced by the increase in the number of banks, financial institutions and insurance companies in the country. It is believed that almost 90% of all new job creation since 2006 has been in the financial services industry.

The country's light manufacturing sector is expanding but with slow speed. Only about 10,000 workers are employed in this area. The semi-conductor industry, for example, has been faced with a global slowdown in demand and been forced to reduce operations. This has also had a negative impact on the local electronics industry whose fortunes rise and fall with semi-conductor production. Other manufacturing activities, especially those in cement and building materials, paint, furniture, chemicals, edible oils and soap have been holding their own.

The agricultural sector has been expanding rapidly, led by increases in sugar and rum production. It should be noted in this context that sugar is not only the most important agricultural commodity produced in the island but that sugar and rum together are the most important merchandise export earners. They also support many industries that are related to the production and marketing of sugar and rum (bottling, labeling, printing, advertising and shipping, just to mention a few).

What is interesting is that sugar and rum production has been expanding. Rum sales have been growing as a result of increased demand for the beverage in North America. Sugar production has been rising, also because of increased world demand, but also due to cutbacks in U.S. based sugar-cane production. The largest sugar-cane producer in the United States, the U.S. Sugar Corporation of Clewiston, Florida, recently announced a planned phase-out of its Florida facilities. Since Cuban sugar is not legally importable into the

States, it leaves a dwindling number of producers in the Caribbean, a boon for Barbadian farmers and exporters.

Under the country's Fiscal Incentives Act, new investments in light manufacturing activities are entitled for up to a15 year tax holiday. These incentives are intended for those manufacturing businesses whose outputs significantly raise the value of employed resources. In addition, businesses producing strictly for export outside the CARICOM area can qualify as International Business Companies (IBC) and be subject to minimal income taxes ranging from 1% to 2.5%.

The Barbados Manufacturing Association (BMA) is the lobby group representing the country's manufacturers. It has been working closely with the government and unions to obtain favorable tax treatment for their members since its inception in 1964. It has also sponsored the island's annual international trade show that showcases Barbadian industry to the world.

The Barbadian manufacturing sector suffers from structural disequilibrium in the sense that it is faced with a chronic shortage of skilled labor and managerial resources. This is due to the fact that skilled and talented local labor tends to seek government jobs that are more secure and offer greater fringe benefits if not higher salaries. And indeed, the public sector is the country's biggest single employer with about half of the labor force working directly or indirectly for the national or parish governments.

There also seems to be more social prestige attached to government service than to the private sector. Sugar and rum and their related industries may be important, but they still carry for some the nasty memories of the plantation era's labor exploitation.

Barbados shares a fundamentally egalitarian and proletarian outlook on life in general that brings its core of socio-economic beliefs closer to the left-of-center ideologies of many socialist societies in the world. In this context, the economics of Barbados cannot be understood without considering the political and economic philosophy of the country's founders and the circumstances influencing their thinking. This "leftist" outlook may be unique to Barbados within the Eastern Caribbean, but it is also mainstream political and economic thought elsewhere in the West Indies, with Cuba, Jamaica, and Trinidad and Tobago being cases in point.

Barbadian history is important in this connection. As mentioned in the *History* and the *Political Environments* section of this book, the people of Barbados evolved since the seventeenth century as slaves and the descendants of slaves in a plantation society ruled by White Anglos who became rich and powerful on the backs of cheap and/or free labor.

The abolition of slavery in 1834 signaled the start of a more than century-long struggle by the emancipated slaves and their descendants against the overwhelming power of the White minority. Little is known of the political and economic philosophies of their early leaders. It is possible that utopian, socialist and communist ideas taking root in Europe, the United States and elsewhere in the Americas in the first half of the nineteenth century may have influenced the beliefs of those early leaders, but little evidence to that effect seems to exist.

What is known is that Grantley Adams, who played a major role in the political life of Barbados between 1937 and 1961, was an Oxford educated Socialist, as were Norman Manley of Jamaica, also Oxford educated and Socialist, and Eric Williams of Trinidad & Tobago (Oxford and Howard University educated). Within their respective lands, they instilled upon their followers over a period of years the idea that society had an obligation through government as surrogate to protect people from life's capriciousness in general by providing an economic safety net and to balance that mission with the need to promote private enterprise to assure growth and development.

Norman Manley, with Alexander Bustamante, another labor leader, guided Jamaica to self-rule and eventually to independence in 1962. Eric Williams, the prime minister of Trinidad and Tobago from 1956 to 1981, had no specific labor interests but he was a dark skinned Creole of humble background and related easily to the plight of poor Blacks. He organized the People's National Movement (PNM) that eventually brought the country's very diverse population together under a national unity banner under the slogan, "nationalism and democracy.... A convention of all and for all.... cutting across race and religion, class and color."

Grantley Adams ties, however, were with the left wing of the British Labor Party, and when he formed the Barbados Labor Party (BLP) in 1938 and the Barbados Workers' Union in 1941, the two organizations adopted British Labor Party goals for their own. A second political party came into existence in 1955 when Errol Barrow, a colleague of Adams, left the BLP to create the Democratic Labor Party (DLP) which won elections in 1961 and 1966 with Errol Barrow as the first prime minister of an independent Barbados.

The two political parties of Barbados, the BLP and the DLP, are closely associated with a number of labor oriented pressure groups and unions. The Barbados Workers' Union (BWU) still exists and is currently led by Leroy Trotman. It is now pert of the Congress of Trade Unions and Staff Associates of Barbados (CTUSAB) which is also led by Leroy Trotman.

The CTUSAB is the umbrella organization for the BWU and also for the Barbados Secondary Teachers' Union (BSTU) led by Patrick Frost, the Barbados Union of Teachers (BUT) led by Herbert Gittens, the Clement Payne Labor Union represented by David Comissions and the National Union of Public Workers led by Joseph Goddard.

These labor groups are allied with the BLP and DLP in shifting alliances that reflect 1 variations of a fundamentally socialistically proletarian theme of maximizing individual welfare under an egalitarian economic system. Some of these ideas were included in the 2008 state of the nation address delivered by Elliot Belgrave, the acting governor-general of Barbados (succeeded by Sir Clifford Straughn Husbands), to the Barbadian legislature, and are summarized below.

1- Improving access to property ownership;
2- Health care for all;
3- Education for all;
4- Treasuring senior citizens in their golden age;
5- Social Security, the Last Safety Net;
6- A full-employment economy;
7- Support for private sector initiatives.

It is interesting that this "wish list" of socio-economic objectives has not affected the recent growth and development of Barbados. Foreign investments have been increasing and building booms in luxury hotel resorts, financial services, data processing centers and light manufacturing facilities are well in evidence, even to the casual visitor. Barbadian society to date has been able to balance its slave-based socialist heritage with modern free enterprise capitalism albeit with slow growth.

Prices must be paid to preserve this balance in a slow growth environment. One is the relative lack of college graduate level and competitive salaried career opportunities in the private sector. This private sector job shortage goes a long way in explaining the high unemployment rate that has stubbornly stayed in the 10% range. This is one reason why the rate of emigration of young people to the United States, Canada and England has kept the rate of overall population growth in Barbados low.

Another price is the social cost of education when executive employment opportunities are limited. Demand for unskilled and semi-skilled labor in the agricultural, tourism and services (infrastructure and facilities maintenance) sectors, but few Barbadians opt for those jobs. Consequently, there has been and continues to be an influx of immigration from less affluent areas to fill the slack. This has created the usual friction that results when old-line residents clash with newcomers who are considered as interlopers despite their importance to the economy.

An increase in government supported social services requires more tax revenue and that has not been happening since the country's tax base is not expanding fast enough to pay for all the programs coming off the drawing boards of the country's economic planners. This has made the country dependent on foreign loans and investments to supplement domestic savings and tax revenues. It was in response to this need for financing that the head of the Central Bank of Barbados, Marion Williams, announced in June, 2008, that it planned to issue at par with a fixed interest annual rate of 6%, interest payable every six months, $100 million in treasury notes maturing in 2016.

A further difficulty is the country's international payments situation. While its reserves of monetary gold and foreign exchange reserves are steady at $620 million, its foreign official debt is higher at $668 million. This shortfall itself is not that serious, but it is being aggravated by the country's high merchandise trade deficit which is not being offset by the volume of incoming investments. To complicate matters, the Barbadian government is committed to maintaining a fixed exchange rate that is currently pegged to the U.S. dollar at 2BBD per USD (the June 30, 2009 rate was 1.99950 bid-ask2.020)./

On a positive note, the Central Bank reported in July 2008 the economy had grown at the annual rate of 4% during the first three months of the year. This compared favorably with the 2.6% rate experienced during the first three months of 2007. The rise in 2008 was spearheaded by an increase in tourism spending and an expansion of manufacturing activity.

The Central Bank was also able to report that as of the end of 2007, the country enjoyed the largest increase in its international monetary reserves since 2000 and was in a position to finance its domestic deficit domestically without recourse to international sources.

V- International Affairs

A motto of Barbados is "Succeeding abroad; winning at home." Barbados, because of its small size, has made it one of its cardinal objectives to become an active participant in international affairs. It has always regarded this full immersion into the political economy of the world as critical to its national security and to its acceptance by the major powers as an important player on the global stage.

Barbados belongs to the Commonwealth of Nations and joined the United Nations the year it became independent in 1966. It joined the Organization of American States (OAS) one year later. It was part of the West Indies Federation from 1958 to 1962, a founding member (1965) of the Caribbean Free Trade Association (CARIFTA) and (1973) of the Caribbean Community and Common Market (CARICOM). The Caribbean Development Bank (CDB), which was created in 1970 and of which Barbados is a member, maintains its headquarters in Bridgetown. Also in Bridgetown is the headquarters of the Eastern Caribbean Security System (CSS). Barbados and six other eastern Caribbean countries belong to the association as well as to the Association of Caribbean States (ACS).

The United States has maintained a cordial political relationship with Barbados even when the island was a British colony and has had a fully staffed embassy in Bridgetown since the country became independent in 1966.. It is said that George Washington visited the colony in 1751, and in fact the United States has had a representative in the country since 1823.

Barbados is considered by the United States important, along with all the other eastern Caribbean states, important to its national security and has maintained a naval base on the island from 1956 to 1978. This is not to suggest that the Leeward and Windward islands are regarded as being of strategic military importance as an armed flank to the concept of a "Fortress America." It is simply that most of the English speaking states in the eastern Caribbean, Barbados included, are fully independent and voting members of the United Nations and it is important for the U.S. to keep them as allies in the global arena of power politics and economic enterprise.

Barbados has been steadfast in its support of U. S. foreign policy in the world. It has in return been a beneficiary of American largesse as dispensed through the Caribbean Basin Initiative, the U.S. Agency for International Development, the World Bank and the Inter-American Development Bank. This quid pro quo has been good for the United States and good for Barbados.

VI- SWOT Analysis

1- Strengths

The major strength of Barbadian society seems to be in the will of its people to convert the country into a diversified and developed high income country. Although its sugar and rum industries are important, light manufacturing, tourism and financial services enhance economic performance and help keep the unemployment rate under control.

Another strength is the existence of a well-educated, skilled labor force that be relied on as the economy grows. These skilled human resources have also been the mainstay of the country's civil service, one of the most professional and competent administrations in the region.

2- Weaknesses

Employment opportunities are not growing fast enough to accommodate all educated and trained Barbadians. A shortage of unskilled and semi-skilled labor requires inward migration from other countries, and creates assimilation problems as foreign labor often has different values. At the same time, Barbadians with marketable skills leave to seek their fortune elsewhere, slowly changing the ratio of

Barbadians to non-Barbadians. The country will eventually need to grapple with the question of what is a Barbadian, an issue of national identity faced by many countries in the world today.

On an equally important note is the overall size of Barbados in terms of geography and demographics. It is geographically small with a small population, little water and sparse natural resources. One wonders if it can ever achieve real economies of scale in anything but sugar, rum, tourism and related financial services. Of course, if these existing assets are efficiently employed, it might be enough to support the economy.

Last but not least is the specter of global terrorism that always looms over the horizon. Tourism declined for several years after 9/11 and began recovering only after 2005. It can suffer again should an act of terrorism strike again.

3- Opportunities

Private sector development in small business enterprise offer excellent opportunities to those with entrepreneurial skills. The burgeoning real estate market is generating demand in everything from banking and construction to insurance and real estate sales. Much of the attraction of real estate stems from the greater number of Barbadians who can now afford to own their own homes and to the increase of high income foreigners who are moving full time or part time to Barbados.

4- Threats

Barbados does not currently face any external political or military threats. Weather can always be a problem during the hurricane season but the country has avoided a serious direct hit in recent years. Of course, climate is unpredictable.

The country maintains good relations with all major world powers and especially with the United States. An unknown factor is the future of Cuba. Should that country repair its political relations with the United States, it might create for Barbados and the rest of the Caribbean a formidable source of economic competition.

VII- Summary and Conclusions

Barbados seems to be one of the better places in the world in which to live, work and play despite its small size. It is also probably one of the world's better managed societies. It ranks # 31 out of 179 countries in the World Bank's 2006 Human Development Index. It is ranked # 23 out of the same 179 countries in Transparency International's Corruption Perspectives Index for 2007. And it is ranked #50 out of 131 reporting countries by the World Economic Forum's 2007-2008 Global Competitiveness Index. There is little doubt that Barbados may be well on the way to reaching its goal of being the world's smallest developed country.

Barbados

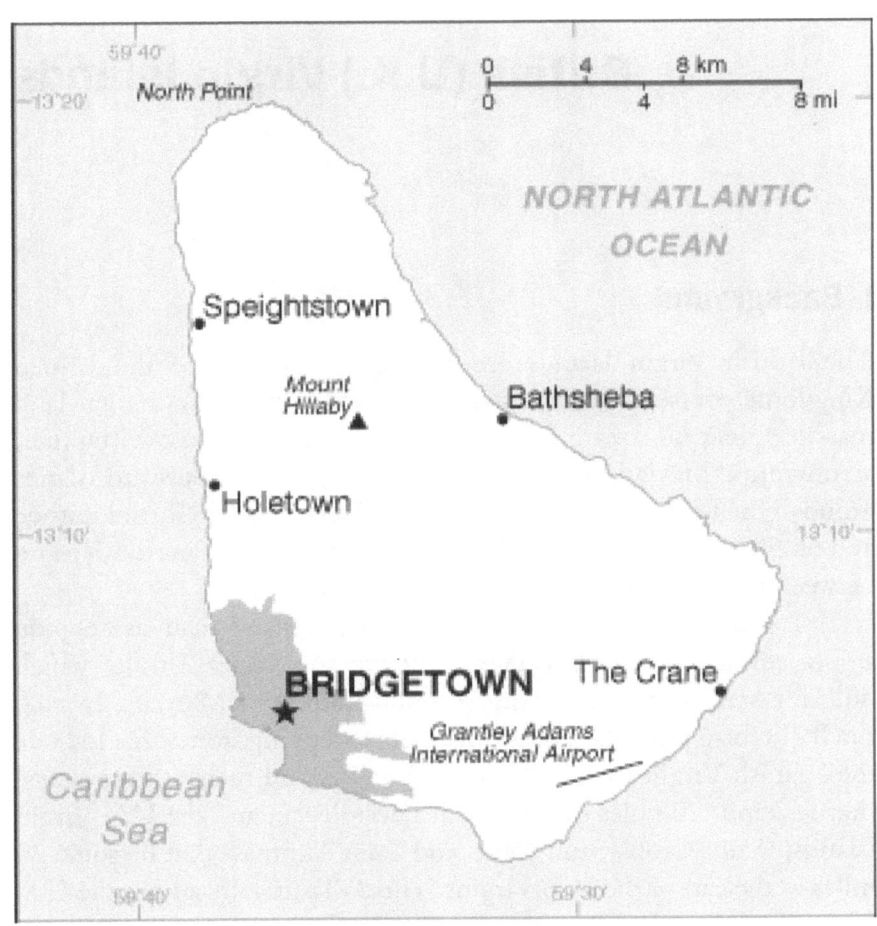

Source: CIA World Fact Book, 2008.

11

British (U.K.) Virgin Islands

I- Background

The British Virgin Islands are among the smaller of the United Kingdom's overseas territories, covering 15 islands with a total land mass of under 60 square miles. They are equally well known by their acronymic abbreviation, the BVI's, and belong to the Leeward Islands group of the Lesser Antilles. Their geo-position is 18.30 North Latitude and 64.30 West Longitude and their location is east of Puerto Rico and between the Atlantic Ocean and the Caribbean Sea. [1]

It is probably more accurate to refer to this island chain as stepping stones connecting the Greater Antilles to the Lesser Antilles which officially start further east with Anguilla and Saint Martens. In fact, the BVI's form part of a much longer set of stepping stones that include the Spanish Virgin Islands (Culebra, Vieques and their outlying cays) that lie about 20 miles to the east of Puerto Rico, and the U.S. Virgin Islands, (Saint Croix, Saint Johns and Saint Thomas) that lie some 20 miles to the east of the U.S. Virgins. The BVI's literally adjoin the U.S. Virgins across a short stretch of water north and east of Saint Johns Island. [2]

The BVI's consist of four major islands, Tortola, Virgin Gorda, Anegada and Jost Van Dyke. Other islands under the jurisdiction of the BVI's include

Beef Island, Cooper Island, Ginger Island, Great Camanoe, Great Thatch, Mosquito Island, Necker Island, Norman Island, Peter Island and Salt Island.

Most of the islands are small and hilly; Anegada is flat, barely visible above sea level. [3]

Road Town, the BVI capital, is on Tortola and is connected to the airport on Beef Island east of Tortola by a bridge. No non-stop flights connect the BVI's to North America or Europe. They are usually accessed by air links from Puerto Rico and by ferry from Saint Thomas in the U.S. Virgins. The BVI's are also a favorite destination of cruising sailors and yachts. It is estimated that over 500, 000 tourists and business travelers visit the islands annually. Many are day trippers from the U.S. Virgins or from cruise ships.

The islands are small. The biggest island, Tortola, is 12 miles long, east to west, and 3 miles across north to south. Their total territory covers less than 60 square miles of hilly land with beautiful beaches and a scarcity of natural water resources. The weather is tropical but trade winds blowing steadily from the east bring cooling breezes. Rainfall varies seasonally but averages 45 inches per year. Most of the water supply is from rainfall and wells and can probably not support a large permanent population. Hurricanes pose a constant threat, routinely sweeping across the BVI's on their way to Central and North America. The land is only 20% arable and traditionally sugar has been one of the few plantation crops it has been able to sustain in the past.

The BVI's combined population is roughly 24,000 as of July, 2008 with about 18,000 living on Tortola in and around Road Town. It is interesting to note that, contrary to trends in the OECS countries, many of which face net population declines due to emigration, the population of the BVI's has been rising at the annual rate of 1.875%. [4]

Tourism and offshore financial services have made BV islanders relatively wealthy. The average annual per capita GDP, purchasing power parity basis adjusted, is almost $39,000, one of the highest in the world. [5] No data for the islands' GINI ratio is available; hence little is known beyond conjecture about the people's distribution of income.

Most BV islanders are of African descent (83%); the rest are White (7%), 5% (mixed), 3% (East Indian) and 2% (so-called other). The majority of the people (86%) are Protestant (Methodist, Anglican, Church of God, Baptist and other denominations). About 10% are Roman Catholics. [6]

II- Historical Environments

It is said that the BVI's were first sighted by Europeans during Christopher Columbus's second voyage to the Americas in 1493. Prior to that time, the islands, like most in the Caribbean, were inhabited by successive waves of immigrants from the Americas mainland. It is argued that Amerindians made their presence known in the islands about 3,500 years ago. Arawak Indians were more recent arrivals, being pushed aside by the more aggressive Carib Indians. [7]

The fate of the Arawaks and Caribs in the BVI's is unclear. One theory is that they were decimated by disease more than by conflict with the European invaders. It is interesting observation that opposition to the Europeans was more pronounced in the southern half of the Lesser Antilles, lasting almost until 1800. Indeed, epidemics, whether brought by Europeans or originating in the Americas, raged from Central America to Canada. This may explain why initial resistance to the Europeans may have been weak in the northern most islands. In any case, Spain claimed the BVI's but never settled them.

For more than a century after Columbus's discovery, the islands were little more than havens for pirates, privateers and general marauders and trouble makers as the major European powers of the age jockeyed for military and political position. The Dutch succeeded in building a settlement in Tortola in 1648, losing it to the English in 1672 while Denmark obtained control over Saint Croix, Saint Johns and Saint Thomas in 1673, keeping them until their sale to the United States in 1914. [8]

The BVI's were not important economically to England, but they were of strategic military significance. The Sir Francis Drake Channel was a long, wide, deep water passage through the BVI's protected by the surrounding islands, making it a hurricane hole and mustering point for the British Navy. From the BVI's, British ships could strike with impunity anywhere in the Atlantic and Caribbean.

In an attempt to make the islands self-supporting, the production of sugar cane was introduced, and by 1700 slaves were imported from Africa and other Caribbean islands to work the new plantations. The sugar enterprise was successful but it could never achieve the large economies of scale and compete effectively with the production capabilities of the larger islands.

The demise of the BVI's plantation system was not due to competition. It lasted until the mid 1800's. It was a sequence of extenuating circumstances that brought its downfall. Devastating hurricanes, competition from the new sugar beet industry in Europe and America and the abolition of slavery in 1834 were the death knells to a social, political and economic order that was built on the back of slave labor.

Slavery explains the racial composition of the BVI's and OECS countries. One John Hawkins passed by the BVI's in 1563 with a slave ship on the way to Hispaniola. It was rumored that some slaves who died on board were left on shore or dumped overboard, but that has yet to be verified. However, it has been recorded that an English privateer attacked a Dutch settlement on Tortola in 1665 and captured 67 slaves who were sent to Bermuda. Holding pens for slaves existed on Scrub and Peter islands. Their remains can still be seen on Peter Island. It is believed that in 1717 there were over 500 slaves in the BVI's. That number grew to about 9,000 in 1788. However, at the time of emancipation in 1834, the slave population was down to 5,000. [9]

Slave revolts were the rule rather than the exception in the BVI's. That is probably a testament to the way in which they were treated. The last major slave revolt was in 1832, two years before the official emancipation date.

Forced into a 14 year so-called apprenticeship, ex-slaves were not fully liberated until almost 1850. The end of slavery coincided with crash in sugar prices, a cholera epidemic followed by a long outbreak of smallpox and two bloody insurrections. These and other developments threw the islands into a state of constant turmoil and ushered in an extended period of stagnation and decline that lasted well into the 1900's. Race relations also deteriorated and almost the entire White population emigrated. By 1893, the only two White people left on Tortola were the deputy governor and a local doctor. [10]

III- Political Environments

The modern political era for the BVI's began in 1967 with the selection of Hamilton Lavity Stoutt to the post of Chief Minister. It was a title reserved for a head of government by England as a colony became self-governing but was not yet fully independent in the determination of its internal affairs. He won four general elections and was the longest serving BVI chief minister.

He did not serve in sequential order, however, and his tenure was broken by constant political bickering that led to the election of two key opponents, Willard Wheatley and Ralph T. O'Neal. Stoutt was nevertheless considered a national hero, and after his death in 1995 a public holiday was declared in his memory. [11]

With the creation of a new constitution in 2007, the old legislative council was dissolved and reconvened as a unicameral House of Assembly. At the same time the title of Chief Minister was up-graded to Prime Minister as part of a process of preparing the BVI's for status as a sovereign nation to enable it to vote and have representation in international organizations and to post embassies within the territory of other countries.

Today, the Queen of England, through an appointed delegate known as the Governor of the BVI's, is technically the head of state and is responsible for the defense and foreign relations of the islands. The Prime Minister is Head of Government and has full responsibility for all internal governance. The current governor is David Pearey (2006) and the sitting prime minister is Ralph T. O'Neal who is appointed by the Governor. By common agreement, however, the prime minister is always the leader of the majority party in the House of Assembly. The prime minister is assisted by an Executive Council (cabinet) whose members are selected by the Governor from members of the House of Assembly. In most cases, the Governor accepts recommendations from the prime minister.

The 15 member legislature is elected by direct popular vote from the nine electoral districts with 4 at large delegates. Therefore, of the 15 members, 9 are elected from their respective districts, 4 are elected "at large," another is is "selected," and one is "ex-officio." [12]

This arrangement is unique to some extent but was intended to address a special situation. Once of the problems faced by the BVI's since local self- government was encouraged by England was that chief ministers and their cabinet members were very often wealthy landowners in their own right, exacting rents from small farmers and merchants. They were also heavily invested in businesses throughout the islands. It was to make the newly constituted government more representative of the general electorate, more democratic and to reduce the influence of cliques and other vested interests that the changes were made. Since political life under the new constitution is about one year old, it is too early to judge the efficacy of this new system of government.

The current majority political party is the Virgin Islands Party (VIP). The largest minority party is the New Democratic Party (NDP). The two parties account for about 85% of all votes. Smaller groups account for the rest. It has not been necessary to date under the new constitution for coalitions to form.

The BVI judicial system is similar to the process followed by the other former English colonies in the Leeward and Windward islands. Judicial decisions in the BVI court system can be appealed to the Eastern Caribbean Supreme Court. Final appeals can be heard by the Privy Council in London.

The present prime minister Ralph Telford O'Neal deserves a mention. He was born in 1933 and was educated at the University of Oxford and studied law. He became an attorney but is not known to have practiced. He instead dedicated his energies to improving his economic position and to a life of politics. The net result was that he ended up being one of the BVI's richest landowners and one of its most powerful politicians. Worthy of mention is the fact that for a while, as he served as a cabinet member on the Executive Council under Hamilton Stoutt's tenure as Chief Minister, O'Neal was also a paid consultant for Royal Dutch Shell. [13]

IV- Economic Environments

It may be historically correct to state that the greatest period of prosperity was during the two centuries when sugar dominated the local economy. And it is true that the sugar plantations generated great income and wealth. But the prosperity was confined to the basically White Anglo plantation owners, the shippers, bankers and insurers. The plantations were labor-intensive and the labor consisted of African slaves and their slave descendants. The fall of commodity prices after 1850 and the presence of several thousands of freed slaves worked to force the BVI economy into a free fall.

This fate was not limited to the BVI's but was experienced by most of the Caribbean islands and the adjacent countries in Central and South America. By 1900, the BVI's, and their Caribbean neighbors, were cursed with a huge labor surplus and a lack of value-adding industries. That fatal combination resulted in the subsistence living and grim poverty that marked the plight of the entire Caribbean as the Second World War approached. Even the war years did little to lessen the islands' economic misery.

It is hard to pinpoint when the economic rejuvenation of the islands began. For the BVI's, and probably for many other islands, the turnaround probably came with the dawn of the jet age. The availability of jet travel coincided with the emergence of a sizeable middle and upper middle class of people with disposable income and more leisure time. That made it possible for people from more developed countries like the United States, Canada and Europe to travel inexpensively and almost with impunity to the far corners of the world.

(Author's Note… When I first traveled to Tortola in the 1950's, I slept on a boat, and there were less than 100 guest rooms on the island. In the 1960's, room availability had increased to over 500. By the 1980's, the BVI's had established themselves as a laid-back destination for tourists and mariners seeking something other than the usual high profile vacations in fast-paced watering holes. By the late 1990's cruise ships began making routine stops in the BVI's. In 2005, according to the CIA World Fact Book, 820,000 tourists spent at least one day in the islands. While most of them were day trippers, 75%, from the U.S. Virgin Islands, Puerto Rico and cruise ships, many were vacationers staying one week or more. It is estimated that in 2007, the BVI's welcomed almost 1 million visitors. I had the pleasure of visiting Tortola a few years ago and was surprised by the changes that had taken place. It had become crowded, noisy, rich and high priced. That may have been good for the BVI's but not so good for me.)…End of Author's note. [13]

With tourism comes money and with money comes the need for banks and financial services. A by-product of financial services is the search by people and businesses for tax havens. The BVI government began promoting what is called "off-shore" corporate and individual registrations that feature the promise of "tax-free" business activity and living as early as the 1980's. It is recorded by the CIA that by 2000, four hundred companies, not including non-corporate entities and individuals, were registered as residents of the BVI's. [14] Wikipedia cites a much higher figure (550,000 companies) but this may be either a typographical error or an exaggeration. Even accepting the lower figure, this "soft investment" inflow together with tourism has provided the islands with a welcome "cash cow." [15]

Very little remains of the BVI's agricultural sector; less than 1% of the labor force is employed in the industry today although it contributes almost 2% to the islands' GDP, testifying to its efficiency and productivity. Sugar is still being grown but it is used in the production of a pricey rum (Pusser's), sold to tourists and exported. Sixty percent of the labor force is employed in tourism and financial services that together produce 92% of GDP. The rest, 38%, work in industry consisting of light manufacturing and maintenance.

The islands' major exports are to the U.S. Virgin Islands, Puerto Rico and the United States, and consist of rum, gravel and sand. Their major imports are automobiles, machinery and just about anything needed to maintain a civilized existence, and their sources of supply are the U.S. Virgin islands, Puerto Rico and the United States. As can be expected, the BVI's sustain a significant and on-going merchandise trade deficit. [16]

It is therefore no secret that the BVI's economic well being depends on its relation with the United States whose residents supply the islands with the bulk of their tourism and financial services income. The BVI's therefore do not use Pound Sterling or the East Caribbean Dollar is the official currency of issue. The currency in common use since 1959 is the U.S. Dollar although most hard currencies are acceptable. [17]

V- International Environments

The BVI's are self-governing islands led by a prime minister as a head of government, but as a United Kingdom dependency they do not post overseas embassies. The latest U.N. General Assembly list of "non-self governing territories" in the eastern Caribbean included the BVI's along with Anguilla, Montserrat and the U.S. Virgin Islands. [18] It is not directly represented in the UN, but it does have associate member status in UNESCO, (the United Nations Educational, Scientific and Cultural Organization) and ECLAC (the UN's Economic Commission for Latin American and the Caribbean). It is also represented as an associate member in the Caribbean Common Market and Community (CARICOM), the Caribbean Development Bank (CDB) and Organization of Eastern Caribbean States (OECS). [19]

There has been some discussion over the years regarding nationhood with full sovereignty for the BVI's, but that idea has not been too enthusiastically supported by BVI's residents who generally believe that their current status gives them the best of all worlds. The islands' "defense" is maintained by England and is supplemented by the constant presence of U.S. naval and air patrols in the region. No pressing international issues face the BVI's and the local government seems to have been content with having its foreign affairs managed by London.

With tourism and financial services being the crankshaft of the economy, the BVI government and business interests have found it prudent to maintain excellent relations mainly through private sector channels with Americans, Canadians, the English and other Europeans. In addition, the BVI's have a cordial working relationship with their Caribbean neighbors and try as much as possible to keep their borders open to make sure that tourists and business travelers can easily enter and leave the islands.

According to the CIA, the BVI's serve as one of the Caribbean points of transfer for the movement of narcotics from South America to the United States and Europe. In all probability, both the UK and US Virgin Islands may be infested with drugs along with the Spanish Virgin Islands and Puerto Rico. [20]

VI- SWAT Analysis

1-Strengths
The main strength of the BVI's lies in their physical proximity to Puerto Rico and to the Spanish and US Virgin Islands, a testament perhaps to the old real estate slogan about "location, location, location." Most non-stop tourist and business travel from the Americas is to

Puerto Rico. Visitors from Europe often fly into San Juan via one of the eastern seaboard air hubs in North America. This has made Puerto Rico the primary destination for millions of people each year who then fan out to other Caribbean islands.

Many will spend their vacations without leaving Puerto Rico. However, as many people will fly to the Virgin Islands for day trips or for more extended stays. This overflow guarantees the BVI's a steady source of income.

San Juan, Puerto Rico, is also a departure port for many cruise ships that make the Virgin Islands (Saint Thomas and Tortola) their first stop. This too assures the BVI's of a continuous income stream.

2- Weaknesses

A possible weakness could materialize if the identity of the BVI's changes from political dependency to fully independent state. It is that dependency that protects the current affluence of the islands. Were the BVI's to remove their velvet shackles, it might be difficult for them to continue enjoying the living standards they are currently experiencing. A more immediate source of weakness is the financial services sector, much of which focuses on the islands' tax haven advantages. More and more countries, the United States included, are cracking down on tax havens in efforts to eliminate tax evasion and avoidance and increase tax revenues. It might be necessary for the BVI government to develop other economy boosting enterprises if eventually tax havens are forced to close their doors.

3- Opportunities

Investment opportunities in the BVI's are largely limited to tourism and related enterprises. Hotel room availability and a scarcity of local power and water supplies are the main issues preventing economic expansion, given that the islands have few other marketable resources besides the weather. In order to capitalize on these opportunities, the BVI's may need to relax its ban on hotel casino gambling.

4- Threats

Hurricanes and storms are immediate threats facing the BVI's as well as all the Leeward and Windward islands. The only anti-dote to violent weather is a higher standard in building construction. A stricter construction code for hotels will need to be adopted before new investments are made in this area.

Earthquakes and volcanic explosions are a constant threat. There are no volcanoes in the BVI's and no earthquakes of note have been recorded in recent history. However, the BVI's exist in a geologically unstable region and natural calamities can never be ruled out.

G- Summary and Conclusions

The BVI's represent a successful transition from a dependent and poverty stricken colony up to the mid 1900's to a prosperous self-governing state. It should also be noted that the islands' political evolution has created a stable constitutional democracy in which all individual rights are protected. It may be convenient to interpret the UN General Assembly's label for the BVI's as a non-self governing territory as a negative characterization, but today that is probably irrelevant to their future political and economic success.

U.K. Virgin Islands

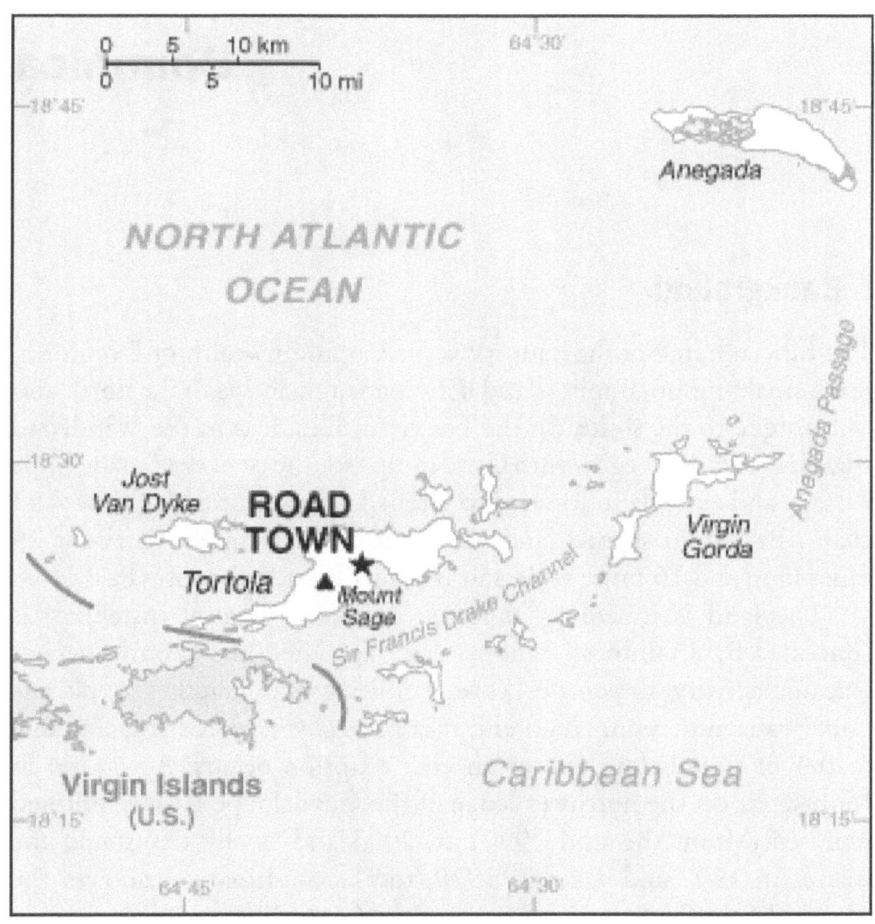

Source: CIA World Fact Book, October 2008 (web accessed 10/23/08)

12
Dominica

I- Background

The official name of the country is the Commonwealth of Dominica. It is a small, mountainous island between Gaudeloupe to the north and Martinique to the south. In the Lesser Antilles, it is in the Windward Islands group that begins with Guadeloupe southeast of the Guadeloupe Passage and extends southward to Grenada at the bottom of the island chain. Its potato shaped land area is 464 square miles, or about 29 miles long and 16 miles wide and is bigger than Barbados. [1]

The land is inherently volcanic but its geological instability is concealed by a rainforest canopy. Although there has been no recent volcanic activity, the entire Lesser Antilles group straddles a volcanic underwater mountain chain and it is generally accepted to be a mere matter of time before one or another eruption occurs. A volcano in Montserrat on the northwest edge of the Guadeloupe Passage erupted repeatedly from the mid 1990's to 2003 and finally devastated the island. In 1902 and again in 1979, the La Soufriere volcano on the island of Saint Vincent just north of the Grenadines erupted, causing thousands of deaths. [2]

Dominica's current population of about 73, 000 live in and around three principal municipalities: Roseau, Portsmouth and Marigot. Roseau is the capital and is on the island's southwest side. Portsmouth is on its northwest side and Marigot on the northeastern side facing the Atlantic Ocean. [3]

The rate of intra-regional emigration and emigration to North America and Europe keeps the rate of population growth low and reduces pressure on the island's existing resources. But a related problem is that it creates a "brain drain" that hinders internal growth and development.

Almost all Dominicans are descendants of African slaves imported by colonial planters in the 18th century. There is also a small Anglo cohort inhabiting the island. Many came as families and couples on cruising sail boats to live out the dream of a simple life in an idyllic tropical island. More interesting is the fact that Dominica is the only island in the east Caribbean in which a small pre-Columbian population continues to survive.

These are the Carib Indians who are said to have arrived in the Caribbean from South America in large canoes in the early 1400's. They displaced the Arawak Indians who arrived earlier from the mainland in the 800's. About 3,000 people claiming Carib ancestry live on Dominica's Atlantic side (east coast) and seem to have become assimilated into the general population. [4]

English is the country's official language, but because it had been a colony of France for a good part of its colonial history, a French patois is spoken by most people. About 80% of the population is Catholic. However, a number of Protestant churches have taken root in recent years. Anglicans outnumber all other denominations which include Methodists, Baptists, Pentecostals and Seventh Day Adventists. [5]

The country is poor in terms of its annual Gross Domestic Product (GDP). Per capita GDP (gross domestic product per every man, woman and child) is estimated to be about $3,800 projected for 2009. U.S. per capita GDP is over $40,000. However, the overall literacy rate is high, about 95%, and average longevity is about 75 years. [6]

And there lies the problem. Dominica is a mountainous tropical paradise with rich land and lush flora, an educated population blessed with long life and very little to do with it. As in most of the other islands in the Lesser Antilles, its main industries are agriculture and tourism, consequences of its environment and history. It is the typical storybook tale of a Garden of Eden that has managed to turn its blessings into curses. This scenario will become more evident in the sections below.

II- History [7]

Dominica's history, like that of most of the West Indies, was a bloody affair until the 1800's. It was tormented before Christopher Columbus's discovery of the island in 1493 and it was strife ridden after. The Arawak Indians seem to have been the first to arrive on the scene. They were either killed or driven off by the Caribs who then engaged in open warfare against the Europeans until they were decimated and marginalized by the English in the early 1800's. The Caribs were an organized and powerful presence throughout the Lesser Antilles, aggressively and successfully resisting European incursions until disease, military losses and attrition reduced their numbers. They were especially successful in Dominica, the island that Columbus supposedly discovered on a Sunday. [8]

Spain was the first European power to try settling Dominica. However, their interest in the island was in mining gold. Failing to find any, Spain lost interest and made no efforts to establish a permanent colony.

The French claimed the island in 1635 and sent missionaries to try to convert the local population to Christianity. They were driven off, creating a military stalemate with the natives that the English tired to break, also with an equal lack of success. A 1660 treaty between England and France agreed to leave Dominica to its own devices, but the Caribs had other ideas and this arrangement lasted only a few years.

If the Cribs lacked anything, it was military technology and know-how. They certainly were not short of aggressive and expansive inclinations. Continuing Carib forays into neighboring islands drove the English to launch an attack against Dominica. In 1674, Philip Warner, a son of the governor of St. Kitts, lead a British force against his half brother, Indian Warner, whose mother was a Carib. Indian Warner had earlier abandoned his English family to return to Dominica as a tribal chief.

Using the pretext of a meeting to discuss an end of hostilities, Indian Warner and his entire Carib tribe were ambushed and massacred on land currently occupied by Canefield Airport. The annihilation of the indigenous population created a labor shortage that was addressed by the importation of slaves from Africa. [9]

It is interesting to note in this context that slavery came to Dominica not from the death of the local Caribs from disease but from military destruction. It should also be noted that their military pacification took 175 years with overpowering force and numbers. A slave based plantation economy was firmly entrenched in Dominica by 1700 and the last Carib holdouts finally ceased their resistance by 1800. [10]

The English tenure was brief. By the 1680's, settlers from Guadeloupe and Martinique established coffee plantations on the island, and by the 1720's, Dominica joined the French West Indies. With the Carib threat and presence reduced, the French and English proceeded to engage in bloody warfare that ended with the island being ceded by France to England under the terms of the Treaty of Paris in 1763. The French tried to retake Dominica on several occasions but finally left the possession firmly in British hands after 1805.

The English replaced coffee with sugar as the crop of choice. Although slavery was officially abolished by Great Britain in 1834, the plantation system remained intact and lasted well into the twentieth century. Indeed, the official end of slavery did not change the life of the former slaves who had little choice but to continue working on the sugar plantations in order to survive.

London created two "federations" for the Lesser Antillean portion of the English West Indies: the Leeward Islands Federation and the Windward Islands Federation. This was part of a plan to groom the English possessions in the Caribbean for eventual self rule and independence.

Dominica stayed with the Leeward Islands Federation until 1939 when its administration was transferred to the Windward Islands group. The island was granted internal affairs autonomy in 1967 and declared an independent republic within the British Commonwealth of Nations in 1978.

Independence has not brought Dominica internal peace. Open violence has never broken out but it has simmered since 1980, and factional strife among competing political groups has been frequent. This ongoing bickering has hampered the island's political evolution and retarded its economic growth and development.

III- Political Environments [11]

Dominica became independent on November 3, 1978. It is a republic with a president, prime minister and parliament and functions as a parliamentary democracy within the Commonwealth of Nations. It has a formally written Constitution although its judicial system follows English common law. The structure of Dominica's government resembles the Westminster style of England's parliamentary system except that it has a unicameral legislature (one chamber called the House of Assembly with 21 regional representatives and nine senators.

Regional delegates are elected by universal suffrage. The senators can be either elected or appointed, the final decision being left to the House. If the appointment route is selected in lieu of an election, the country's president can name five senators with the advice of the prime minister and four with the advice of the leader of the opposition party. If the election route is chosen, senators are selected through a vote by the regional representatives. However, elections for the House must be held at least once every five years, but the prime minister can call an election at any time.

Dominica's president is nominated by the prime minister in consultation with the leader of the opposition party and is elected for a five year term by the parliament. The president in turn appoints the leader of the majority party in the House as prime minister.

He also appoints cabinet ministers subject to the prime minister's recommendation from the ruling party. The president, prime minister and cabinet constitute the government's executive branch. They are accountable to the parliament and can be removed on a no-confidence vote. Elections are held on the basis of universal adult suffrage.

The judicial branch has magistrates and jury courts linked by appeal to the Eastern Caribbean Supreme Court (High Court and Court of Appeals) and to England's Privy Council. The country is divided into ten subdivisions called parishes which are responsible for most governance within their territorial jurisdictions.

This is where Dominica's political problems begin. The parishes, each with their own local governments, are political sub-divisions. They preside over the towns and villages within their respective jurisdictions and exercise considerable influence over the national government. Councils elected by universal suffrage govern most towns and are supported by property taxes, much of which remains within the parish system. Consequently, each parish has the power to govern its domain as a feudal fiefdom.

The central government, because of the country's political organization, is too sensitive to mood changes in the local parishes. This has proven to be divisive, placing too much emphasis on local issues and blurring focus the more pressing economic problems of growth and development. Hence, the island's political parties, the Dominica Labor Party, the Dominica Freedom Party (the current coalition partners), and the United Workers Party (the opposition party), often find themselves in a quarrelsome quagmire of internal disputes and seem unable to agree on a national economic policy.

IV- Economic Environments [12]

Much of Dominica's adult population between the ages of 18 and 65 is engaged in the agricultural sector. Services (tourism and the public service) and commerce accounts for 30% and 20% of the workforce respectively. The unemployment rate, one of the highest in the West Indies, ranges between 25% and 30%.

In general, Dominica's economy has stagnated for years. Although rich in agricultural resources and in agricultural output, domestic and foreign demand for them is low. It has timber, water for hydropower and copper, but the island mass is too small and its ecology is too fragile to allow development to acceptable economies of scale.

The agricultural sector, organized around a small scale commercial plantation system, produces bananas, citrus, cocoa and coconuts, and accounts for 17% of GDP. It is most noteworthy that while agriculture accounts for 37% of the workforce, its contribution to GDP is much lower.

Agriculture, with bananas as the principal crop, is still Dominica's economic mainstay. Banana production employs, directly or indirectly, over one-third of the work force. This sector is vulnerable to weather conditions and to external events affecting commodity prices. A related problem is that almost every sub-tropical and tropical country produces bananas, a commodity crop for which the foreign elasticity of demand is quite elastic. It is a global industry engaged in perfect competition that has little power to raise prices.

In view of the European Union's (EU) phase-out of preferred access of bananas to its markets, agricultural diversification has become a priority of national policy. Dominica has made some progress and now exports citrus fruits and vegetables. It has also gone into coffee, patchouli, aloe vera, cut flowers, and exotic fruits such as mangoes, guavas, and papayas.

Dominica has had even more success in developing its manufactured exports, with soap as the primary product. It has more recently entered the offshore financial services market but it is too soon to predict the success of that endeavor.,

There is manufacturing activity, mostly in the area of agricultural processing, but that generates only about 8.5% of GDP. The tourism oriented service sector has the greatest potential for growth. However, there are to date only about 800 rentable rooms spread among small guest houses and hotels scattered throughout the island.

Dominica's volcanic geology has produced few usable beaches. Therefore, tourism has been slow to develop compared with progress made in that activity on other neighboring islands. Nevertheless, the country's mountains, rainforests, freshwater lakes, hot springs, waterfalls, and diving spots attract the eco-tourist and cruise ship stopovers have risen following the construction of modern docking and waterfront facilities in the capital.

The growth of the tourism industry has been hampered by two factors, location and marketing. The country's size and geographic location has historically discouraged the major airlines from initiating direct or non-stop flights from the metropolitan centers of North America and Europe. This has placed Dominica beyond the interest and reach of the conventional tourist limited to a one or two week vacation. Tourism marketing has been another constraint. Large cruise ships today routinely cover all the islands on a weekly basis. Not only has this diverted income from Dominica; it has also dampened popular demand for land based hotel facilities and discouraged investment in modern, full service hotels.

Finally, Dominica's small economy has made it difficult to budget funds for effective advertising campaigns to attract visitors. Hence, tourism is limited to a relatively few intrepid individuals and families seeking experiences that are different from the mass markets of the larger West Indian islands. Dominica had nearly 205,000 tourist visitors in 2002, with nearly 15,000 stay-over visitors from the U.S. Cruise ship passenger arrivals in 2002 totaled 136,859. It is estimated that 4,500 Americans reside in the country.

Dominica's international trade reflects the mercantilist arrangements of the colonial era when more industrial countries used the islands as sources of raw materials in exchange for finished, manufactured goods. To this day, the country exports its agriculture and semi-processed goods and imports manufactured articles for domestic consumption. As of 2005, Dominica exports about $50 million and imports $100 million. It trades with its CARICOM neighbors, but most of its commerce is with North America and the European Union.

V- International Affairs. [13]

Dominica maintains friendly relations with most countries. It belongs to the Eastern Caribbean Currency Union (ECCU) and is a member of the Caribbean Community and Common Market (CARICOM) and Organization of Eastern Caribbean States (OECS).

The Eastern Caribbean Central Bank (ECCB) issues a common currency to all eight members of the ECCU. It manages monetary policy and regulates the banking activities of its member countries. Although Dominica is included in the Caribbean Basin Initiative (CBI) of the United States, economic progress has been modest at best. In terms of its trade, the country imports twice as much as it exports, and with no significant offsets from incoming foreign investments, it is deeply in debt.

The main thrust of Dominica's foreign relations is economic growth and development. To this end, it maintains missions in Washington, New York, London, and Brussels and is represented jointly with other Organization of Eastern Caribbean States (OECS) members in Canada. Dominica also is a member of the Caribbean Development Bank (CDB) and the British Commonwealth. It joined the United Nations, the International Monetary Fund (IMF) and the World Bank (IBRD) in 1978, and became a member of the Organization of American States (OAS) in 1979.

Good relations with the United States have had some salutary results. In exchange for Dominica's support, the U.S. helped Dominica to expand its economy. U.S. assistance is currently channeled through agencies such as the World Bank, the Caribbean Development Bank (CDB), and through the U.S. Agency for International Development (USAID) office in Barbados. The Peace Corps provides technical assistance through 30 volunteers who work in education, youth development and health services projects.

Much of the support requested by the United States is in the war on illegal drugs and Dominica participates in programs to control drug trafficking and marijuana cultivation. It signed a maritime law enforcement agreement with the U.S. in 1995 to strengthen counter narcotics coordination, and signed mutual legal assistance and extradition treaties to enhance joint efforts in combating international crime in 1996. [14]

VI- SWOT ANALYSIS

1-Strengths. Dominica's greatest strength is its brand of constitutional democracy that has endeavored to establish orderly and representative government under a rule of law. It is also blessed with warm weather that makes it attractive to tourists seeking a tropical vacation. It also has an abundant flora resource base that can be developed into a niche market for toiletries, cosmetics and specialty foods.

2- Weaknesses. The country is too small to be a major economic and political contender in world affairs and global enterprise. Although it is an active member of many regional organizations such as CARICOM, it has yet to receive significant benefits from its active and long standing associations. A poorly developed internal infrastructure and a relatively weak communications and transportation system increase the difficulties of attracting the investment resources needed for achieving sustained economic growth.

3- Opportunities. Tourism offers the greatest immediate opportunity for accelerating the country's economic growth and reducing its high unemployment rate. Dominica already receives many visitors annually who arrive on cruise ships. While this is noteworthy, the cruise ship tourists spend less than a day on average on land, denying the economy the revenues it would normally receive from overnight visitors. Increasing room capacity will therefore be necessary if tourism is to be a more viable industry. This will involve large scale investments in hotel construction and all related tourism related services. What will also be needed is an expansion of airport facilities and a dramatic increase in the number of direct, non-stop flights from Europe and North America.

4- Threats. Dominica has no external enemies. The only threat it faces is its internal divisiveness in terms of a lack of focus on achieving economic growth objectives. There is to date scant evidence of concerted policies and programs by the government designed to turn the country's environment from a economic backwater into a more dynamic and progressive society. This economic retardation is seen here as a significant threat to the small nation's continued independence.

VII- Summary and Conclusion

Dominica has yet to make real economic progress to catch up with some of its neighbors in the region. Its reliance on agriculture, public sector services and an aging infrastructure renders it globally uncompetitive. Investments in private sector industries that pay higher wages and add value to the economy are needed. Concentration on low wage, labor intensive enterprises such as agriculture and small scale manufacturing are insufficient to raise wages and material well being. Dominica remains today an economic backwater, albeit a stable one, depending on foreign assistance and caught in a neo-colonial time warp.

The World Economic Forum has no global competitiveness ranking or score for Dominica. [15] Transparency International's Corruption Perceptions Index ranks the country as #37 out of 179 countries with a score of 5.6. [16] The World Bank's Human Development Index ranks it as #71 of 177 countries with a score of 0.798. [17

Dominica

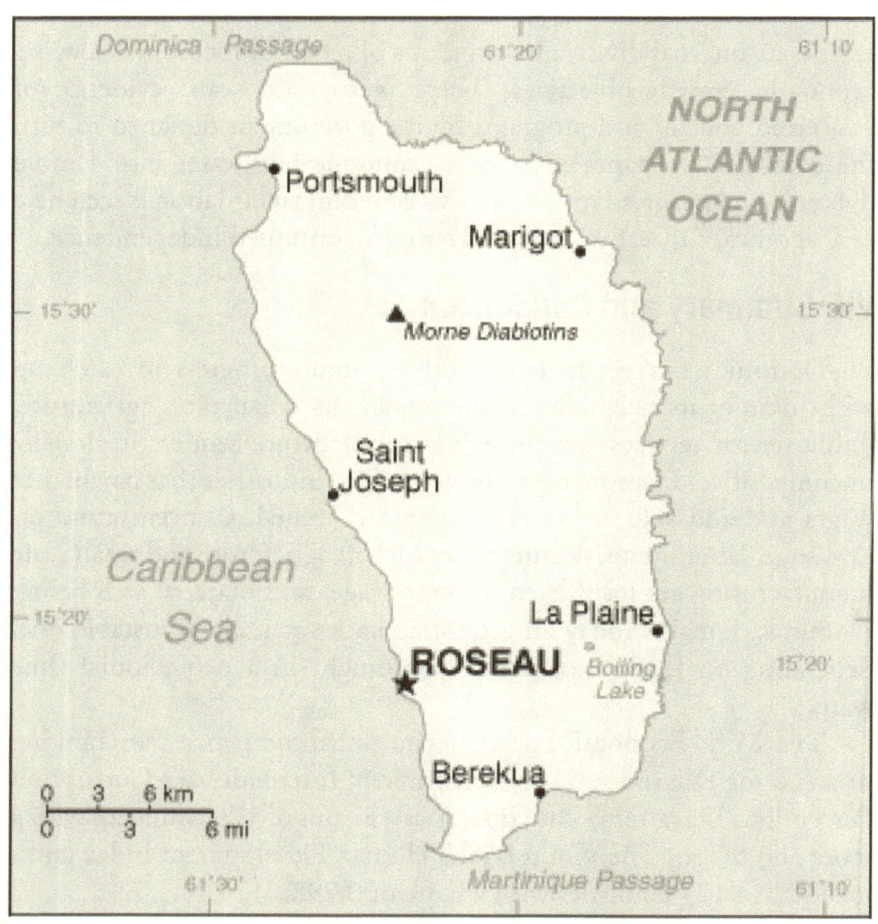

Source: CIA World Fact Book, 2008.

13

Grenada

I- Background

This nation is the most southern of the Windward Islands that form part of the eastern Caribbean and are members of the Organization of Eastern Caribbean States (OECS). It is situated north of Trinidad and Tobago and south of Saint Vincent and the Grenadines. It, and its two major adjacent islands and assorted smaller cays, cover 133 square miles of land, making its total land size about 30% greater than that of Nantucket Island. The main island of Grenada itself is only about the size of Nantucket. The two adjacent islands are Carriacou with 13 square miles and Petite Martinique with 483 acres. Both are about a one hour ferry ride north from St. Georges, the capital and main port of Grenada. And between them and Lavera Beach at the northern tip of Grenada are a string of tiny cays that attract cruising sailors, yachters, water sports enthusiasts and vacationing tourists. South of Tyrrel Bay at Grenada's southern tip, are more tiny cays that provide stepping stones for part of the way to Trinidad and Tobago. [1]

The islands are volcanic in origin and there is still an active submarine volcano south of the island of Granada called "Kickin' Jenny." The terrain is quite hilly. Grenada's tallest mountain is Mt. St. Catherine at 2,756 feet from which waterfall filled rivers cascade into the sea. The land's volcanic nature has rendered the soil so fertile that anything amenable growing in a tropical or semi-tropical environment thrives well in Grenada. [2]

The country has always relished the fact that it lies south of the hurricane zone. Its luck turned sour in 1955 when it was severely struck by Hurricane Janet. Hurricanes struck again in 2004 and 2005, again causing considerable damage. There have been no severe storms since that time. The possibility of damage from inclement weather is important to consider because repairing the damage wrought exacts a greater percentage toll from an emerging market's income than it does from a larger and wealthier country.

Grenada and some of the Grenadines have historically been known for their spices and called the "Spice Islands." Grenada in particular is called the "Spice Island, being famous for its nutmeg and other spices. In fact, Grenada is an important producer of mace, cinnamon, cloves, ginger, allspice and orange and citrus peel, and currently supplies over 20% of the world's consumption. [3]

The combined population of Grenada is 110,000 with over 90% of the people living on the main island. Most of the rest reside in Carriacou, a tourist destination in its own right. The great majority of the people are African slave descendants. Due to the high rate of emigration, it is thought that Grenadians living in Europe and North America outnumber those in Grenada. The Carib Indians have all but disappeared from Grenada, having been annihilated by the French in the 1600's. There are a few East Indians whose ancestors came as indentured servants in the 1800's and tiny English and French communities that have survived from the early colonial days.

English is the official language but a French patois can still be heard on the streets. Most of the people are Protestant, many being Anglicans, and there is an active Catholic minority coexisting with smaller religious groups. [4]

Grenada is not a rich country in terms of its GDP and accurate and recent data is hard to come by, but in 2002, its average annual per capita GDP was reported at $5,000. There is reason to believe that it has gone up over the years and that it may today be in the $6,500 range. [5]

Public health standards also seem to leave room for improvement. Average longevity at birth, as reported by the World Bank, is 68 years, one of the lowest in the East Caribbean. [6]

II- History

The Spanish did not fare well in their confrontations with the Carib Indians when they attempted to settle the island in the early 1500's. They were followed by the English who also failed. The French purchased Grenada in 1640 and planted a colony, "La Grenade" for the purpose of producing sugar. It had a large, natural harbor on the southwest side where the French built a fortified port, "Fort Royal." It proved to be an excellent port of refuge and hurricane hole and the French navy used it often as a haven for their ships in heavy weather. [7]

But the real problem faced by the French was not the weather. Neither was it having the labor necessary for their plantations; slaves and forced labor provided the workforce. It was the Caribs who successfully pinned the French down behind their fortifications not only in Grenada but also in Dominica and St. Vincent. The French, determined to wrest control of at least Grenada from the Caribs, brought in reinforcements from Martinique and engaged the Amerindians in a series of pitched battles with overwhelming military force and numbers.

The last battle was fought in 1651 and it ended in victory for the French. The surviving Caribs, men, women and children, retreated to a cliff at the northern tip of Grenada and jumped to their deaths. The hill on which the Carib community committed mass suicide is shown as Sauteurs (Leapers) or Carib's Jump on local maps and has become a national landmark. The French lost Grenada to the English in 1763, regained it in 1779 and lost it again in 1783. England retained control over Grenada until its independence in 1974. [8]

Although sugar was the crop of choice in the 1600 and 1700's, nutmeg, cocoa and other spices soon became the preferred cash crops from the 1800's to the present time. This was a fortunate transition for slaves working the giant plantations because spices can be cultivated in smaller tracts of land that lend themselves to small farm agriculture. With the abolition of slavery in 1834, former slaves were more easily able to transition from forced to free labor with many ex-slave families becoming small land owners in the spice business.

Grenada as a colony had no government of its own from 1833 to 1958 and was administered by the British Windward Islands Administration that had dominion over St. Lucia, Saint Vincent, the Grenadines, Dominica, Trinidad and Tobago and Barbados. The island group was officially called the Federal Colony of the Windward Islands. Its seat of government was Barbados until 1885 when the island became a stand-alone colony. The seat of government was then moved to Trinidad and Tobago until 1940 when it was transferred once again, this time to Dominica under a new name, the Territory of the Windward Islands. The colonial confederation was formally dissolved in 1960. [8]

Even before the confederation died, Grenada jumped ship and joined the new West Indies Federation, a political and economic confederation that had been promoted and painstakingly designed for several years by England and larger West Indian colonies like Jamaica and Barbados. It finally came into being in 1958 amid much hope and fanfare, only to be dissolved in 1962 when it became clear that many islands, having experienced a taste of full self-government, were psychologically unprepared for the power sharing required in a political federation. [9]

Immediately upon the demise of the West Indies Federation, Trinidad and Tobago, along with Jamaica, Barbados and the other more highly populated states began shaping the architecture of what was to become a limited trade bloc or free trade association called the Caribbean Free Trade Association or CARIFTA which officially went into operation in 1965. At the political end of the spectrum, England went ahead and introduced the fairly novel concept of "associated statehood," implying that such a country could enjoy full self-government as a member of the Commonwealth of Nations under the British crown as head of state. It was under that arrangement that Grenada earned full independence as a sovereign nation in 1974. [10]

As in the case of other eastern Caribbean nations, the head of state is the English crown that appoints a governor-general to represent the monarch and the English government. Grenada's first prime minister was Sir Eric Matthew Gairy, but his tenure was short lived and ushered in a long period of bloody strife and political turmoil. The problem was that his politics were far to the left of center and he promoted Cuban involvement in Grenada's economy. That led to a land redistribution program that faced resistance from the general population, unhappiness in Washington and resulted in an armed revolt. [11]

Gairy was deposed and replaced by Maurice Bishop who was himself removed from office in 1983 and placed under house arrest despite his immense popularity. He was subsequently set free but was soon arrested again and executed summarily by soldiers who also executed several other government ministers. Peace was restored when the United States sent a military force to restore order. This period in Grenada's history remains an open sore in the country's internal politics and also in its relations with the United States.

III- Political Environments

The political structure of Grenada is that of a parliamentary constitutional democracy like all the other English speaking eastern Caribbean countries. The head of state, as indicated earlier, is the monarch of the United Kingdom, presently Queen Elizabeth II, represented on site by a governor-general who is appointed by the crown. The head of government is a prime minister who is technically appointed by the Queen through the governor-general upon the recommendation of the political party or parties in power. Usually, the prime minister is the leader of the majority political party or the leader of a coalition of parties. The prime minister governs with the help of a cabinet of ministers selected from the majority and minority parties. [11]

Party members are elected to serve in a legislature ("Parliament" in Grenada) through periodic general elections every five years held in the country's six parishes, St. Andrew, St. David, St. George, St. John, St. Mark and St. Patrick. The Parliament is composed of a 13 member Senate and a 15 member House of Representatives. Senators are appointed by consensus between the government and the opposition parties. Representatives are elected for five-year terms by the electorate in the six parishes. [12]

This overall organizational formula devised by England for its former colonies evolved over many generations and was intended, as it did for the other countries in the region, to guarantee peace and stability through an orderly transition of political power from one competing group to another via scheduled elections. This formula initially failed in the case of Grenada.

Indeed, the seeds of revolution were planted soon after independence in 1974, and in 1979 a Marxist revolutionary by the name of Maurice Bishop and a band of followers known as the New Jewel Movement took over the country while the real prime minister was in New York City addressing the United Nations. This was followed by an armed uprising in 1983 and with United States military intervention to restore order and the government to power. Memories of those chaotic years where one prime minister was deposed and another executed without trial are still disruptive points of argument in Grenada today. [13]

It is hard to imagine how matters could have deteriorated to the point of open warfare and bloodshed in Grenada so soon after independence without appreciating the dynamics of its society and of the outside pressures it faced in the 1970's and 1980's. Grenadian society was neither very rich nor very poor, and most of the people lived at or only slightly above the poverty or subsistence level. But they had managed to survive nevertheless.

The great sugar plantations were long gone by 1900, having been replaced by smaller landholdings whose proprietors concentrated on spice cultivation. These were mostly families with strong, well established feelings of small business entrepreneurship. Allied to them were the shopkeepers, merchants and traders who worked through banks and large international trading companies to market their output overseas. To borrow a phrase from the time of the French Revolution, they were the bourgeois capitalists, or, "la petite bourgeoisie," as they were called in France. Highly individualistic in their personal lives, they nevertheless depended on the government to institute policies that would protect and promote their interests. They added up to about a third of the adult work force, and their politics tended to have a conservative slant to the right of center.

Another third of the work force consisted of Grenada's population that was more highly educated (many with college and graduate degrees) and steered away from entrepreneurial pursuits. Most of this group found employment in government administration, law enforcement, teaching in the K-12 grades or even in colleges and technical schools, program and project administration for government works and in private sector careers. Their politics leaned left of center and they were philosophically comfortable with the last third of the work force with whom they formed any number of political alliances and associations,

Workers in this last third of the Grenadian labor force were generally less educated, poorer, and were the ones who toiled physically for a living and in general did the "heavy lifting" of society. Their leaders' convictions were on the far left of the political center and many were Socialist or Communist or even Marxist in their orientation.

This great divide created a slightly bi-polar society that was nevertheless united in the pursuit of somewhat center-left political and economic goals, namely, capitalism with a strong dose of social welfare, or socialism with a strong dose of capitalism. From a regional perspective, the parliamentary constitutional democracy that was working so well elsewhere in the English speaking Caribbean should also have worked well in Grenada. And that did seem to be the case in the beginning.

The country's first chief minster prior to full independence, and who then became prime minister, was a Grenadian born career politician (1920), Eric Matthew Gairy, who served between 1967 and 1979. He was a pragmatist whose sole objective in life seems to have been the pursuit of his country's leadership. He was labor oriented by background and formed a union that he soon turned into a political party, the Grenada United Labor Party (GULP), that had the widespread support of the business and farming community.

He was fascinated to an extent with Fidel Castro's Cuba and sought out its economic assistance when support from financial support from England and the United States was lagging. This meant that the U.S.S.R., through Cuba as a surrogate, began funding the country's economic growth. Soon Cuban doctors and teachers were a daily presence in Grenada and rumors began to circulate that Gairy might be flirting with the idea of turning the country into a communist state.

But that was not Gairy's aim. He wanted Cuba's aid but not its ideology to advance the interests of his political constituency. He easily won re-election in 1976, but was accused of election fraud by a relatively younger man and fresh face on the scene, Maurice Bishop, who led a new political party, the New Jewel Movement. He was young, brash and impatient and could not wait for the next election to throw his lot against his aging opponent. Hence, he staged a coup with his supporters and Gairy was forcibly overthrown in 1979. Grenadian politics were fractured for years to come as a result.

Maurice Bishop had a different agenda. He was born in 1944 to Rupert and Alimenta Bishop who were wealthy enough and sufficiently well connected to send him to the London School of Economics where he studied the black power movement which was in the process of spreading beyond the United States. His combined interest in black power and Marxist ideology turned him into a revolutionary.

When he returned to Grenada, he joined an upstart revolutionary group as a community organizer. This association that went by the acronym, JEWEL (Joint Endeavor for Welfare, Education and Liberation), was a hotbed of activity that attracted many young firebrands like Bishop who were filled with ideas and energy but little political and administrative experience and very limited knowledge of regional and global power politics.

In short, JEWEL was a Leninist-Marxist organization wholly dedicated to the takeover of Grenada by peaceful and/or violent means, in other words, by whatever worked. A political party called the New Jewel Movement or NJM sprung out of JEWEL and Bishop soon won a seat in the parliament. He became NJM party leader and devoted his tenure to opposing almost every move and recommendation made by the Gairy government and GULP. Further, without official authority, he created a secret paramilitary unit that operated under the JEWEL umbrella. The unit eventually became known as the National Liberation Army (NLA) or "Twelve Apostles." This last name was a reference to twelve men who were secretly sent to Guyana for guerilla training in anticipation of staging a coup to take over the country.

Bishop's timing was perfect. In a surprise move that caught Grenada and most of the world off guard, he and his followers took over the government while Matthew Gairy was at the United Nations in New York City giving a speech. The NJM and NLA seized the reigns of government and Bishop had himself appointed to the post of prime minister, to the consternation of other Caribbean states and of course much to the concern of the United States.

While he was head of government, all political parties were banned except for the NJM and elections were cancelled. Laws were arbitrarily passed by decree by Bishop or his party's inner circle organized in a central committee called the People's Revolutionary Government (PRG) in which his mistress, Jacqueline Creft, had a ministerial post. One of the first orders of business was to shut down the judicial system.

He nurtured the close relationship with Cuba to enlist its help in building a new airport in the south and to turn the NLA into a large army, the People's Revolutionary Army (PRA). Funding for the airport came from the USSR via Cuba but the design came from European contractors. PRA recruits took a loyalty oath to the NJM and Marxist Socialism as the basis of government.

The new administration was now ready to seize property and to implement land seizure and redistribution programs and was well on the way to turning the country into a totalitarian Marxist dictatorship. What was interesting in the brief height of his power was that Bishop enjoyed mass popular support. His land reform policies and programs were aimed mainly at the remaining plantations whose owners had long become disenchanted with revenues generated from commodity agriculture. Spices were good but they did not make or break the economy and few new fortunes were being created from their cultivation and exportation. Grenadian entrepreneurs were happy with their businesses and did not see Bishop as a threat to their endeavors. Indeed, many relished the fact that at last he might bring to the country much needed infrastructure investments, even if it meant that they came from Cuba and the USSR. And of course, to the manual labor work force, Bishop was the hero who brought them employment, income, health care and schools. The problem was not what he did but how he did it, by violent revolution rather than through an orderly electoral process.

What brought Bishop down was an internal dispute with members of the NJM who could not agree among themselves on policy matters. Opposition NJM members placed him under house arrest in October, 1983, but he was to popular and an outpouring of public opinion forced his release. His first move upon being released was to enlist military assistance in an effort to bolster his position, but his return to power was brief. He was in the process of meeting with a number of political leaders when they were suddenly set upon and arrested. Most of them were immediately executed without a trial by a firing squad.

There was a sad footnote to the Bishop saga. In 1966, he had married one Angela Redhead in 1966 with whom he had two children,

John and Karin. His wife left for Canada in 1981 with their children while he was still prime minister but after he started his affair with Jacqueline Creft, a minister in his cabinet, with whom he also had a son, Vladimir. Unfortunately, Jacqueline was executed along with Bishop and his other companions. Vladimir was killed in a stabbing in Toronto a few years later.

Maurice Bishop was succeeded by Hudson Austin, another revolutionary and member of the NJM, who issued shoot to kill orders to enforce a curfew. His government fell less than a week later when the United States invaded Grenada on October 25 after rumors that American medical students at St. George's University School of Medicine might be at risk began spreading.

Austin and others who were responsible for the killing of Bishop and his entourage were arrested and brought to trial. Hudson Austin is still in prison.

Matthew Gairy returned to Grenada and tried to make a political comeback but was unsuccessful. He died in 1997. His GULP party won 2 seats in the House of Representatives in the 1995 general election and won nothing in the 2000 elections. By sheer luck, a member of the leading New National Party defected to the GULP, giving it a lone seat. Gloria Payne Banfield was the GULP leader in 2003, becoming the country's first female party leader. In the 2003 general elections, GULP won 3.2% of the popular vote but no seats. It tried a coalition for the July 2008 elections with the People's Labor Movement and still won no seats.

The New National Party (currently lead by Keith Mitchell) has a definite conservative bend. It came into being in 1984 through a merger of the Grenada National Party (Herbert Blaize), the National Democratic Party (George Brizan) and the Grenada Democratic Movement (Francis Alexis).

The NNP won 14 0f 15 seats in 1984 and Blaise became Prime Minister. Blaise lost to Mitchell in an intra-party squabble and Mitchell led the party into the 1990 elections and lost all but 2 seats. After a number of zig-zag victories and defeats, the NNP lost the 2008 elections to the National Democratic Congress with Tillman Thomas as the current Prime Minister.

It is interesting to note that the U.S. invasion of Grenada, Operation Urgent Fury, however short lived and surgical, was poorly received by other regional states and England. It was also condemned by the United Nations. However, Grenada has been peaceful and stable ever since the heady days of the early 1980's and its democratic institutions have been functioning well.

The disruptive years of the Bishop era were subjects of a new investigation between 2002 and 2004 by a "truth and reconciliation" commission under the chairmanship of a Roman Catholic Priest, Father Mark Haynes. It came to the conclusion that many Grenadians were still bitter about the disputes and divisiveness that brought about the rebellion and continue to believe that the injustices that Matthew Gairy and Maurice Bishop tried to resolve, each in his own way, have not yet been addressed.

IV- Economic Environments

The completion of the Point Salines International Airport, started by the Cubans in the 1970's, marks Grenada's inadvertent entry into the tourism industry with a positive turn-around in the country's economic growth and development beginning in the mid-1990's. The new airport and jet travel made the country more readily accessible to business and pleasure travel from North America and Europe and helped bring about a rapid rise in the number of visitors.

Tourism is today Grenada's fastest growing economic sector, having passed agriculture as the leading earner of foreign currencies. Although the country is an important source of supply for spices, bananas, cocoa and citrus fruits, it does not have enough arable land to accommodate economies of scale that would make those products more competitive in world markets. There is, however, some doubt as to whether tourism can ever create enough income to accelerate the country's economic growth and development and to significantly raise living standards.

The country has greatly expanded its part facilities at St. George's to allow four large cruise ships to dock daily with each vessel carrying 2,000 to 3,000 passengers. This is now having the impact of creating much needed revenue for St. George's and its outlying areas. The docks are filled with cruise ships about three days of out of the week with each ship arriving in the morning and leaving in the late afternoon or by early evening. Weekend ship traffic is negligible since cruise ships generally start returning to their home ports by Friday.

Two week cruises allow one weekend at a tourist hot spot destination, but that to date has not been Grenada. The downside of cruise ship tourism is that passengers spend most of their money on board and relatively little on land, even when they get to go on shore.

This raises the issue of on-land resort hotel facilities. About 25 full service hotels are in operation in Grenada and Carriacou that can accept about 2,500 individuals and/or families nightly. There are a greater number of boutique hotels and small inns but they barely double the number of available rooms or suites.

Grenada is one of the more attractive and diversified tourist attractions in the entire Caribbean but it needs to expand its facilities. The problem is that large scale investments in new hotels are not being made by the major hotel chains. One reason for the shyness of foreign investments inflows has been the political and economic uncertainty in the world since the 2001 terrorist attacks on the U.S. Another reason has been the unpredictable climate. The area has been battered by hurricanes in the recent past and has barely had enough time to recover. Moreover, recovery has been slow and costly.

Any progress the country has made in advancing its economy has often been offset by unfortunate extenuating circumstances and skyrocketing budget deficits. The economy has been growing nonetheless, but so has the country's public debt which is today over 200% of its GDP. To aggravate matters, Grenada is import dependent, importing more merchandise than it exports. This merchandise trade deficit is not countered by net inflows of private foreign investments, forcing the government to borrow heavily to finance its international payments deficits.

Grenada's currency is the East Caribbean Dollar which is pegged to the U.S. Dollar at 2.7 EC$ per US Dollar through its membership in the Eastern Caribbean Central Bank (ECCB). In the final analysis, this currency peg can only be held with support from the United States and other hard currency nations. [14]

The European Union and the United States account for 40% and 24% respectively of Grenada's exports. Barbados, St Kitts and Nevis and St' Lucia are its other important customers. Grenada's major foreign suppliers are the United States (43%), Trinidad and Tobago (19%), the European Union (12%), Japan (5%) and Barbados (3%). [15]

V- International Affairs [16]

England struck a symbolic blow at the importance it felt for Grenada when it closed its embassy in St. George's in 2006 and transferred its services to the High Commissioner's office in Barbados. It was in fact an economy and convenience move which had nothing to do with any attitude change or any change in the political relationship between the two countries. But it still had to have been a blow to the ego. Today, the High Commissioner's Barbados office has the responsibility for representing the United Kingdom throughout the region. However, China, Cuba, the United States and Venezuela all have embassies in Grenada. Although most of the English speaking eastern Caribbean nations have recognized Taiwan, Grenada has not, opting instead to have diplomatic relations with the People's Republic of China.

It is a member of the usual international organizations (The United Nations, the World Bank, the International Monetary Fund and the World Trade organization). It is also a member of the Caribbean Development Bank, the Organization of American States and the Eastern Caribbean Regional Security System.

Grenada is a beneficiary of America's Caribbean Basin Initiative and the United States Agency for International Development and the Peace Corp. It also cooperates with the United States on military matters and in trying to stem the flow of narcotics from South America.

There are about 2,600 Americans currently residing in Grenada, not including the 2,000 American medical students attending St. George's University School of Medicine.

VI- SWOT Analysis

1- Strengths
Natural beauty, balmy weather and a friendly population are strengths that can help the country move its economy forward as it becomes a popular destination for vacationers. As a consequence, it is making a great effort to expand its hospitality industry.

2- Weaknesses

As in Saint Vincent and the Grenadines and many other islands, the country's natural resources, its fertile soil and rich forest land, are both strengths and weaknesses. These resources in the past have served to attract low cost, unskilled and semi-skilled workers to labor-intensive occupations at a great profit to landowners. Perpetuating this weakness is the country's relatively large population which makes it all the more difficult to rapidly convert a low wage society into higher salaried workers.

Another weakness is the inadequacy of domestic savings and the lack of international financing for investments and infrastructure. This situation hampers the introduction of large economy of scale industries catering to foreign markets that can quickly raise local incomes through higher wages and salaries. Tourism has excellent potential for expansion but it needs more investment, infrastructure and facilities for its potential to bear fruit.

3- Opportunities

Expansion into light manufacturing enterprises is an area of interest that needs closer scrutiny. The increase in tourism is generating demand for new hotel construction, and that in turn has created a boom in the construction industry which has raised demand for construction equipment and supplies. The heavy machines can be imported, but much of the smaller equipment and many of the supplies can be produced locally as some already are.

Diversification into value-adding industries begets economic growth and development. Investments and investment financing are important here, but the availability of skilled human resources is more important. These are already in place in Grenada.

4- Threats

Hurricanes have become real threats and obstacles to sustained economic growth for Grenada. These have repeatedly struck the country with devastating results. The country has an active offshore submarine volcano but it has not posed a threat lately. What may happen in the future is unpredictable. Natural events are unpreventable, to be sure, but stricter construction codes are being enforced by the Grenadian government and that should help minimize damage when disaster strikes again.

VII- Summary and conclusions

Grenada, like Saint Vincent and the Grenadines, is anxious to shed its banana republic image. It seems to have at long last been able to make its institutions of constitutional parliamentary democracy work over the long term and that may help Grenada develop the ground work to create a globally competitive market economy. However, democracy does not guarantee economic growth. The economic challenge for Grenada is a regional issue that must be shared by all the English speaking Caribbean states. They are too small to be a viable international force. Greater cooperation, participation and reciprocation in the existing regional organizations will be necessary if the individual member countries are to make genuine long term progress.

The World Bank ranks Grenada as No. 82 in its Human Development Index (HDI) with a score of 0.777 and classifies it as a medium income country. [17] The country is ranked No. 79 in Transparency International's Corruption Index with a score of 3.4. [18] This implies that corruption may be an issue that impacts its capacity to grow its economy. [19] It has not yet been rated by the World Economic Forum's Competitiveness Index.

Grenada

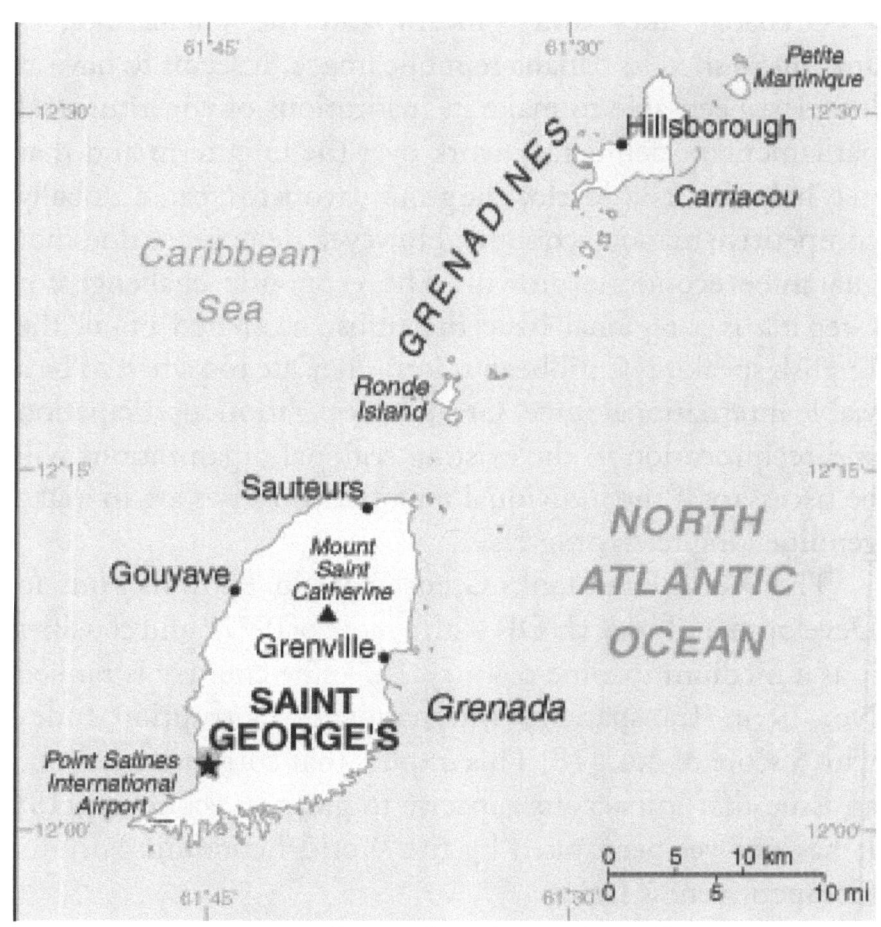

Source: CIA World Fact Book, October 2008 (cia.org/library)

14

Montserrat

I- Background

Montserrat is an example of how an act of nature, a volcanic eruption this time, has been able to bring the progress of civilization to an unexpected halt in recent memory. The world is not blind to the serious interruptions that can be caused by natural calamities. Death and devastation caused by hurricanes, earthquakes, floods and volcanic action sweeps across the planet constantly with unrelenting fury. However, in this past generation, catastrophes, terrible as they were, never destroyed the material infrastructure of an entire society. The erupting Soufriere Hills volcano in 1995 was different. It brought life in Montserrat to a standstill from which its people have never recovered. [1]

Montserrat is a small island, 7 miles across and 10 miles long, of about 40 square miles of irregularly shaped hilly land with a protruding volcano rising over its southeastern hills and peering down upon Plymouth, the capital until 1995. (It was moved temporarily to the Brades estate after the eruption).

It is 300 miles east-southeast of Puerto Rico and 30 miles southwest of Antigua. It is a pretty island, somewhat arid, often called the Emerald Island of the Caribbean because of its light green color from a distance and because many Europeans who settled there were of Irish descent. Its geo positioning is 16.45 North Latitude and 62.12 West Longitude. [2]

About 13,000 people lived on Montserrat before the 1995 eruption. Half of the population lived in or around the old picturesque town of Plymouth. This number has reportedly dropped to more than half since the disaster. What is interesting about the Soufriere volcano is that no record exists of its having ever erupted and it was considered dormant. (Author's note: I sailed around the island in July of 1991and visited Plymouth from Antigua several times before then. I knew of the mountain's existence but was unaware that it was a volcano. Of greater concern to me were the hurricanes that had a habit of barreling through the islands during the summer months. And sure enough, Hurricane Andrew began its trip across the Atlantic in August, but I was in the Biminis when the storm threatened and in Fort Lauderdale when it struck). About 4500 people live on Montserrat today.

It was fortunate for the islanders that Montserrat kept its connection to the United Kingdom as a British overseas territory. This link placed the people in line for speedy assistance when the volcano blew. Indeed, the mountain began shaking and spewing weeks before its great eruption. This gave more than sufficient time for people to be evacuated from the island in an orderly fashion.

Plymouth was destroyed as a direct consequence of the eruption and the entire southwestern sector of Montserrat was abandoned. A resettlement program moved residents to the island's northeast sector, but much of the population never returned. It is estimated that today about 5,000 people live on the island.

The Soufriere volcano has not been inactive since 1995. The last recorded incident of a mild tremor and eruption occurred in 2003. (Author's note: I sailed past Plymouth in 2005. The lingering odor of hydrogen gas in the air reminded me that the volcano was alive and well and I photographed smoke over the mountain's dome). In May 2006, the dome collapsed and showered ash over the island. No further incidents have been reported to date.

Montserrat's demographic makeup reflects the island's ethnic composition and racial underpinnings. The population has Black and White components but much of it is mixed of Irish and African descent. Religious preferences also follow these historical influences. A full 40% of the people are Catholic and another 40% are Protestant, with most being Anglican and Methodist. The rest are classified as "other" and include Pentecostals and Seventh-Day Adventists. Over 90% of the population is classified as being of African descent, attesting to its centuries of institutionalized slavery.

II- Historical Environments [4]

The first Europeans encountered by the native Arawak and Carib Indians in Montserrat were the Spaniards in 1493. The island was fought over by the Spanish, English and French until 1632 when England finally took control to protect a rag-tag band of Irish settlers migrating in from St. Kitts and Nevis. The practice of slavery was institutionalized by 1650 to supply labor for the new sugar and cotton plantations and forced labor was imported from both Africa and Ireland. A fascinating feature of slavery at its start in Montserrat is that slaves came from both Africa and Ireland. Oliver Cromwell, when he took power in England in 1648, used the exportation of Irish Catholics as slaves to the Caribbean and specifically to Montserrat, as a means of ridding Great Britain of religious undesirables. The Celtic influence on Montserrat culture has been lasting. To this day, Saint Patrick's Day is a legal, official holiday on the island.

In any case, the French wrested control of the island from the English in 1782, only to turn it over to them the next year as part of a treaty. Slavery, as elsewhere, required severe repression and considerable time and effort was spent in quelling uprisings. When England, as the 1700's came to an end, found itself in control over Montserrat and over much of the islands of the West Indies, it found itself saddled with supporting a sugar plantation system based on slavery whose profitability had flattened and whose costs were rising. In Montserrat specifically, the small size of its plantations meant that sugar cultivation could not achieve the economies of scale and compete successfully with the much larger tracts of the Greater Antilles or with the other more populated islands of the Eastern Caribbean.

Slavery was abolished officially throughout the British Empire by England in 1834, preceding a gradual collapse in global commodity prices, including the price of sugar. Hence, the emancipated slaves of Montserrat became all of a sudden a new under-class of free people unable to find work because of a simultaneous decline of the plantation system.

It was the philanthropy of Joseph Sturge in 1869 whose company bought up idle sugar plantations for the production of limes that gave new life to the island. Profits from lime cultivation were used locally to purchase additional land that was subsequently divided into smaller lots and re-sold to the local population, including the former slaves and indentured servants/ This is why today Montserrat is mostly a land of small landowners who survive on the basis of subsistence agriculture, cottage industries and considerable foreign assistance from more prosperous donor countries.

England consolidated its Caribbean colonies in 1871, creating a Leeward Islands Federal Colony through which Montserrat was governed until 1958 when it joined the West Indies Federation in 1958. The Federation was dissolved by its members in 1962 and Montserrat later joined the OECS (Organization of East Caribbean States) as one of England's self-governing territories. It has from within the OECS experimented with several forms of cross-border association with neighboring states, but none have proven any better than others in helping the island move its economy forward.

This is because Nature has not been kind to Montserrat in the past decades. Hurricane Hugo passed directly through the island in 1989 with devastating effect. Wind and rain tore through 90% of existing buildings and it took the better part of the next five years for the people to recover. No sooner was the hurricane a memory when the Soufriere Hills volcano erupted, burying the south side of the island and Plymouth under ash and lava. Strenuous efforts were made at first to recover from this disaster, only to be thwarted by a new sequence of explosions. These culminated with an eruption in 1997 that cost the lives of a number of people and led to the abandonment of any sustained recovery and reconstruction effort. The last major eruption was in 2003.

III- Political Environments

The seat of local government used to be Plymouth. It was moved to the Brades estate on Montserrat's northwest end after 1996. The move was to have been temporary, but Brades remains today the state's de facto capital. The political system is a constitutional democracy on the English model, and since Montserrat is an English overseas territory, it has a chief minister but no prime minister, as a head of government. The English crown is the head of state and is represented a governor appointed by London. The present Governor is Peter A. Waterworth (as of July, 2007) and the Chief Minister is Lowell Lewis (since June 2006). [5]

The Executive Council functions as a cabinet led by the Chief Minister. Its members are the Governor, Chief Minister, attorney general and the finance secretary. Three more ministers serve on a rotating basis.

The eleven member legislature is unicameral (one house) and nine of its members are elected at-large every five years. The attorney general and financial secretary are ex officio members and occupy the last two seats. Prior to 2001, members of the legislative were elected from their individual parishes. This was changed to a voter-at-large system in which the voter was given the right to vote for a slate of nine candidates of his or her choosing.

The Montserrat electorate is active and turnout at the polls is always high.

The vote split in the 2006 election was 36.1% for the Movement for Change and Prosperity (MCAP), 29.4% for the New People's Liberation Movement,

24.4% for the Montserrat Democratic Party (MDP) and 10.1% for those who voted "independent." [6]

The distribution of legislative seats was interesting. The MCAP received 4 seats; the NPLM garnered 3 seats, the MDP and Independents together had 1 seat apiece. This meant that the MDP and Independents could band together with the attorney-general and finance secretary to form a four-vote bloc that could be a tiebreaker if two more votes from the dominant parties could be picked up.

Montserrat's judicial system has a local court system from which appeals may be taken to the High Court. The High Court is tied to the OECS judicial system which has its own Supreme Court in St. Lucia and to which decisions may be further appealed. A judge from the Supreme Court and Montserrat resident presides over the island's High Court.

IV- Economic Environments

With its current population estimated to be at 4,500, and with the Soufriere Hills volcano still smoking, Montserrat's economic future seems bleak. Its population growth rate is understandably static and average longevity from the time of birth is s about 72 years. The island's annual per capita GDP for 2002 was estimated to have been $3,400. More recent data was unavailable for this book. It is suspected, however, that with the overall economy is in a state of slight decline and has been so since 1995. [7]

The country's economic growth potential, whatever it might end up being, is locked to volcano action. Although Montserrat is now in the process of receiving over $100 million in assistance from England to repair its damaged infrastructure, the prospect s for private investment inflows to stimulate the economy for the long run appear slim. A new airport opened on the island's northern side in 2005, but its capacity is limited thus far to short distance inter-island flights.

V- International Environments

Montserrat's major export markets for hot peppers, limes and some cattle are the United States and Antigua. Imports are much higher than its exports, and its major sources of foreign supply are the United States, Trinidad and Tobago, Japan and Canada. Principal imported items are machinery, fuels, transportation equipment and processed foods.

As a member of the OECS, Montserrat's currency is the East Caribbean Dollar (XCD) which is pegged to the US Dollar at 2.7 XCD per US$. The rate has been fixed since 1976, but as a practical matter it, like most East Caribbean dollars, is not easily convertible because of limited demand.

Montserrat is also a member of the East Caribbean Central Bank (ECCB) that coordinates the monetary policies of its members. Finally, it belongs to the Caribbean Community (CARICOM) along with all other West Indian states.

Montserrat

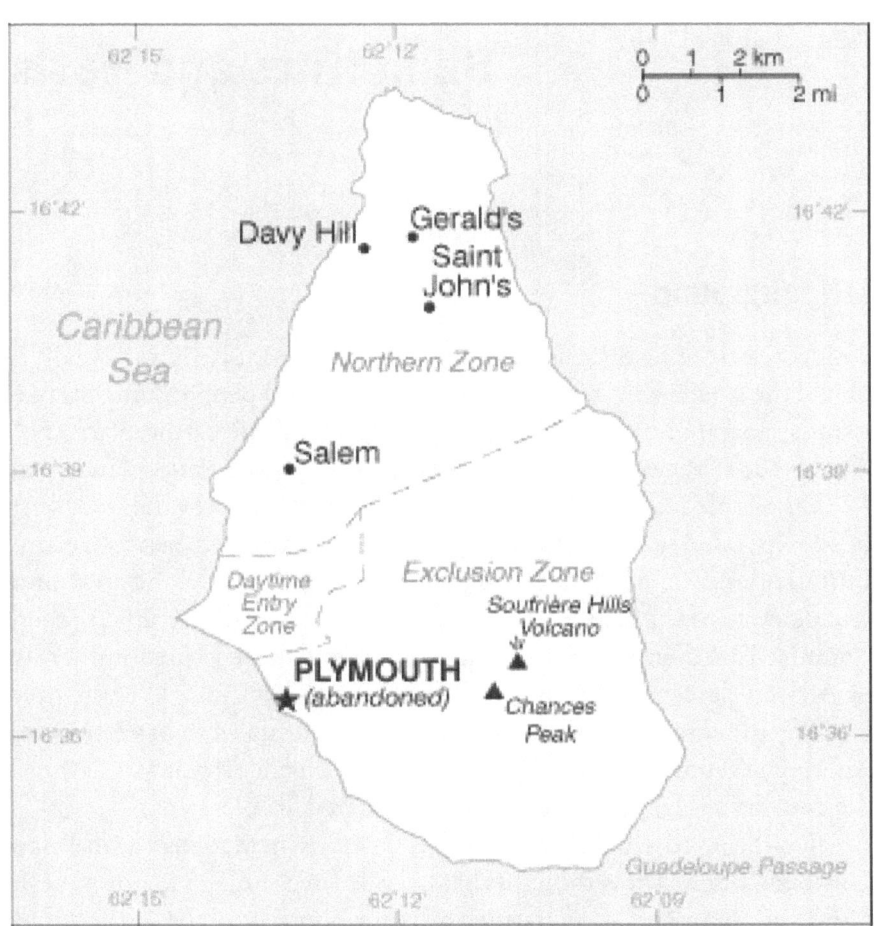

Source: Central Intelligence World Fact Book, October, 2008 (web accessed on 20 October, 2008).

15

Saint Kitts and Nevis

I- Background

This country, officially called the Federation of Saint Kitts and Nevis, is one of the smallest in the world with about 42,000 people living on two islands separated by a shallow two-mile channel called "the Narrows." About 30, 000 people live on St. Kitts, a 65 square mile island, and 12,000 people reside in Nevis, a 36 square mile island to the southeast of St. Kitts. Geographically, the country is sandwiched between Saint Eustatius and Saint Maarten to the northwest and Montserrat and Guadeloupe to the southeast. The two islands together are smaller than Catalina Island in California and their population is predominantly of African descent. The country's total population in 1960 was over 51,000, the loss since then being attributed to high emigration rates. An update reported by the U.S. Central Intelligence Agency (CIA) has the country's July, 2008, population estimated at 39,619. [1]

It is believed that Christopher Columbus named the island San Cristobal, but it is now thought that he called at Sant Jago (Saint James). However, the island was classified as San Cristobal by the 1600,s, and when the British finally took possession, they simply called it Saint Kitts. The etymology of Nevis followed a similar eclectic evolution. It was originally named for Nuestra Senora de las Nieves (Our Lady of the Snows) until it came finally to be known simply as Nevis. [2]

The people of St. Kitts call themselves Kittitians, and those from Nevis are referred to as Nevisians. Ninety percent of the people are

Black; 5% are mixed; 3% are East Indian and 2% are White or "Other." The majority religion is Anglican, followed by other Protestant denominations, Catholics and a few Rastafarians. [3]

Small as it is, the country has played a significant role in the history of the Caribbean and it has not been without its celebrities and celebrity events. The 2007 Cricket World Cup had some of its competition games played in the country, and Nevis is also the birthplace of Alexander Hamilton. Horatio Nelson was stationed in Nevis when he was young, and that was where he met and married Frances Nisbet, the young widow of a plantation owner. The island nation, in its colonial prime, was a major sugar producing center in the Caribbean and played a significant role in the slave trade. Its history has also been checkered, buffeted as was in the 1600 and 1700's by England and France in their constant wars with one another. Today, the country endures a shaky union, having barely survived a secessionist movement by Nevis. [4]

It is, perhaps of its small size and excellent climate, relatively prosperous. Average annual per capita GDP is officially reported at about $16,000, and that may be under-stated. Average longevity at birth is 75 years, and adult literacy is almost 100%. The tourism industry dominates the economy today, supplemented by some agriculture and light manufacturing activities that are geared mainly to supporting the infrastructure of the country and its many hotels and tourist attractions. [5]

The country, although not geographically remote, cannot be easily reached by direct flight from the North American or European mainland (there are a few direct flights from the eastern seaboard of the United States), although it is accessible by cruise ship and is included as a day stop on many itineraries. Aside from cruise ship traffic, it is a vacation destination for enterprising and wealthy travelers who come to savor the sights, the weather, food, ambiance, service and great hospitality and are willing to pay the high prices.

The two islands were once volcanic and are therefore quite hilly except for the coastal lowlands where Basseterre, the capital on St. Kitts Island, is situated. The highest elevation in the country is on St. Kitts, Mt. Liamuiga, at 3,793 feet. It is an extinct volcano whose crater is a tourist attraction.

II- History [6]

A Carib tribe called the "Kalinago" had already been inhabiting the two islands when the Europeans arrived. They were less aggressive than the Caribs in the larger islands and were more receptive to European intrusion. Unfortunately, the Europeans who settled the islands did not distinguish the difference between the peaceful Kalingo and their warlike Carib cousins.

A group of French Huguenots attempted a settlement on the north coast of St. Kitts but were soon driven off by the Spanish. Captain John Smith stopped briefly in Nevis in 1607 on the way to North America (Virginia) but he never planted a colony.

At about the same time, Thomas Warner, another British adventurer and explorer, set about exploring the north coast of South America for suitable land for a colony. Weather conditions strange to him and his crew, tropical diseases and hostile Caribs destroyed his hope of establishing a permanent colony in Guyana and forced him to sail north to the eastern Caribbean where he finally came upon St. Kitts in 1624 where he had a simple port village built around a deep water basin at Old Road. The French arrived in 1625, as a coincidental result of having come out second best with a Spanish naval force, and were invited by the English to land and settle in Nevis. Most of the French, however, stayed in St. Kitts.

News of these settlements soon reached the Caribs throughout the neighboring islands and they planned an attack with the connivance of the Kalingos to expel and/or destroy the Europeans. Word of the plan leaked out and the English and French forces combined to launch a preemptive strike against the Kalingos in 1626.

What followed was a night ambush at night followed by the massacre of every native on the two islands. It became known as the Kalinago Genocide of 1626, and the area where the fighting took place and where thousands of Indians died was named Bloody Point and Bloody Point River.

The Kalinago Genocide marked the end of a native Indian presence in St. Kitts and Nevis.

The Kalingo Genocide ushered in a brief period of cooperation between the English and French during which time they shared control over St. Kitts and Nevis and used the islands to consolidate their hold on other eastern Caribbean possessions. The peace between the English and French ended by 1630 after a Spanish raid leveled much of St. Kitts. First, the English and French fought off the Spanish and then they started fighting each other. Control over St. Kitts shifted several times between England and France until the end of the 1700's when St. Kitts became a permanent English colony.

St. Kitts jumpstarted its economy with tobacco which soon became the cash crop of choice. However, competition from Virginia tobacco shut down the industry and the St. Kitts plantations switched to sugar in 1640. And since sugar cane production is much more labor intensive, and there was a shortage of labor, the slave trade began flourishing.

While life in St. Kitts was uncertain in the 1600's, Nevis prospered. In 1628, a resident of St. Kitts, Anthony Hilton, and eighty followers moved to Nevis to grow tobacco. In 1640, they too shifted to sugar. Within a few years Nevis was England's most profitable colony on a per capita basis in the Western Hemisphere. It never relinquished its position until the early 1800's when slavery as an institution was falling in disfavor and sugar was being grown more efficiently and productively in other countries.

Sugar production was briefly interrupted in 1690 by an earthquake and tsunami that destroyed Jamestown, the existing capital, and many of the plantations. However, the sugar industry recovered and the capital was moved south to the town of Charlestown.

St. Kitts fortunes took a turn for the better in the 1700's and soon the two islands had the distinction of being Great Britain's most successful ventures in the Caribbean. For reasons which still remain to be researched St. Kitts and Nevis were always able to turn misfortune into an opportunity and land on their feet.

For example, a series of French raids on the sugar plantations in Nevis destroyed the industry in the late 1700's and brought the local economy to its knees. The enterprising Nevisians recovered by building a luxury tourist residence called the Bath Hotel near one of the island's fabled hot springs. Soon, wealthy travelers from England and even from France were visiting Nevis on a regular basis, and in short order Nevis became a popular destination. To this day, Nevis has the distinction of having the first tourist resort in the Western hemisphere.

The end of slavery in 1834 and decline of the sugar industry in the eastern Caribbean brought St. Kitts and Nevis and their neighboring islands into relative eclipse. But it also served to galvanize the sugar workers into a cohesive labor organization to force the various colonials and post colonial governments to seek economic policies and programs that would increase employment, income and living standards. The formation in 1833 of the Federal Colony of the Leeward islands and, later in 1883, of a single "presidency" to preside over St. Kitts, Nevis and Anguilla (with its center in St. Kitts), although disliked by many of the people in the Leewards, gave the mostly non-White labor force a chance to form alliances beyond their island borders.

The demand for independence, generally encouraged by England as the 1800's slipped into the 1900's, merged with the cry for economic emancipation, an idea that fitted in well with England whose economic philosophy was also moving left. By the 1930's, the concepts of constitutional government under a limited monarchy and equal economic empowerment for all had gone mainstream in St. Kitts and Nevis as they had in much of the English speaking eastern Caribbean.

St. Kitts and Nevis was granted full autonomy in 1967 and full independence in 1983, making it the newest nation in the Western Hemisphere. Nevis attempted constitutionally to secede and form its own country in 1998, but a referendum vote fell short of the two-thirds majority needed for a legal separation.

III- Political Environments [7]

The country is a member of the Commonwealth of Nations and is totally independent. It recognizes the British sovereign as Head of State through a governor-general appointed by Queen Elizabeth II. The head of government is a prime minister who is usually the leader of the majority political party and shares power with a National Assembly which, in the case of St. Kitts and Nevis, is a unicameral legislature of 11 elected representatives (three being from Nevis) and three senators appointed by the governor-general. Two of those three are recommended by the prime minister and one is selected by the leader of the opposition party.

Two political groups have dominated the political scene in St. Kitts and Nevis since the early 1900's, the Labor Party (LP) and the People's

Action Movement Party (PAM). While both parties can take credit for ending the islands' colonial status, it was The LP led Robert Llewellyn Bradshaw that guided the colony on its long road to independence. He governed the country as prime minister until his death from prostate cancer in 1978.

He was and remains one of the more prominent of West Indian leaders to have been at the forefront of national independence movements in the area. He was born in 1916 on St. Kitts in the town of Saint Paul Capisterre and was educated on the island where he eventually became a labor activist. He

was a supporter of labor causes and was forever sensitive to sugar workers who were among the country's lowest wage earners.

Sugar had been the focus of economic and social thought and action for two centuries, even though its profitability had been declining for years. Plantation owners, who had by now diversified their investments, clung to generations-old beliefs that were still tinged with racism. A number of these even sold their real estate holdings to foreigners who had their own plans and had little interest in the sugar industry, let alone to participate in its rejuvenation.

Matters came to a head in with the world economic depression of 1929. In 1930, world sugar prices collapsed. Economic paralysis in the colony provided the momentum for its labor movement to come together. Robert Bradshaw saw his opportunity and organized the Workers' League in 1932 that became involved in the colony's 1935-36 labor riots that had already been spreading like wildfires throughout the eastern Caribbean between 1934 and 1939.

The riots, although violent and bloody, were inconclusive and proved nothing. But it gave Bradshaw another opportunity to cement his position with the labor movement. In 1940, the Workers' League morphed into the St. Kitts and Nevis Trades and Labor Union which formed its own political party, the St. Kitts and Nevis Labor Party. It was strong enough by 1946 to help elect Bradshaw to the local legislature. The LP went on to control political life in the two islands for three decades with Robert Bradshaw at the helm.

He went on to serve as Minister of Finance, Chief Minister and finally as Prime Minister, a position he held until his death in 1978. During his tenure his true colors emerged as a left wing socialist who believed in state ownership in the assets of production. During his tenure as prime minister, the sugar lands and the sugar refineries were bought by the government which gradually adopted a policy of control in one form or another over almost all business enterprises. Further, Bradshaw progressively changed from a labor activist to an imperious, high handed bureaucrat.

Opposition to the LP grew, especially in Nevis, and had he lived, he probably would have lost his post. He was succeeded upon his death by Paul Southwell who died a few months later. The LP was defeated by the PAM in 1980 which remained in power until 1995 when power once again reverted back to the LP led by Denzil Douglas who to date is still the prime minister. Two more parties have surfaced in the past ten years. These are the Concerned Citizens Movement (CCM) led by Vance Amory and Nevis Reformation Party (NRP) led by Joseph Parry. The CCM is beginning to gravitate towards the PAM and might impact the next general election results. The NRP is interested in having Nevis become an independent nation in its own right.

IV- Economic Environments [8]

Tourism is now the country's major source of income and its principal earner of foreign exchange. It has also focused its attention on light manufacturing industries. This has had positive results thus far. A thriving wearing apparel sector has materialized and the island nation boasts one of the largest electronics assembly operations in the region.

Two problems exist for these activities, as they do for tourism and almost anything else in the eastern Caribbean. The first is that St. Kitts and Nevist has too small a population to offer a market for anything but small, cottage type, family owned businesses where it is possible for producers to make slightly more than a subsistence living.

Micro financial services such as banking and insurance can be successful among small populations but expansion is difficult unless the savings rate increases and people have extra money to invest elsewhere. Additional income must therefore come from industries that achieve larger economies of scale by catering to bigger markets abroad. And here, profitability is predicated on the size of those foreign markets and their ever-changing demand picture.

Health care is a good example of this problem. The country has excellent public health facilities and human resources to offer and provide high care standards at the individual and community levels and has world class out-patient treatment clinics, but it is not in a position to offer full service hospitals specialized in potentially catastrophic ailments as are available in much larger population concentrations. Insofar as the wearing apparel and electronics industries are concerned, these cater mostly to larger overseas markets and become subject to economic, technological and cultural changes abroad.

The second problem is climate. Hurricanes and storms, not to mention geological events like earthquakes, volcanic eruptions and tsunamis do tend to wipe away from time to time, but within minutes, much of the economic progress that has painstakingly been pieced together to create a decent standard of living for residents. St. Kitts and Nevis did well in the 1990's until back-to-back hurricanes struck the islands in 1998 and 1999. To worsen matters, the terrorist strike of September 11, 2001, at the United States brought tourism and most businesses in the islands to a standstill. The country has been making a comeback but those earlier events and the cost of rebuilding have left it deeply in debt.

An unfortunate consequence of seemingly insoluble problems has been an outbound flight of the country's better education young adults. This "brain drain" has accounted for a net population loss sustained by the islands for at least a generation. The government and private sector has yet to find the formula to retain its better qualified citizens.

The government today is burdened with a public debt that is about 200% of its GDP and shows little chance of being reduced any time soon. Much of the debt is due to losses sustained by public sector ventures into economic enterprise, but of it has resulted from the fact that government expenditures, however well intended, are not matched by the necessary revenues.

Although tourism is the country's chief source of income, the industry is too limited in scope to really grow the economy in the long term. It is reported that 341,000 tourists visited St. Kitts and Nevis in 2005 with that figure possibly rising to over 400,000 in 2007. Over half of all visitors are day-trippers from cruise ships and neighboring islands, thereby limited their contribution to the country's economy.

The country's merchandise exports of $84 million are meager compared to its imports of $383 million in 2006. Final data for 2007 is unavailable to date but evidence suggests that this trade deficit will continue. St. Kitts and Nevis exports food, beverages, tobacco, machinery and electronics to, by order of importance, the United States, Canada, Europe (Netherlands) and Azerbaijan. It imports manufactured goods, processed foods and fuels from, by order of importance, Trinidad and Tobago, Spain and the United Kingdom.

As do most English speaking eastern Caribbean countries, the official currency is the East Caribbean Dollar (XCD) which is pegged to the U.S. Dollar at 2.7 XCD to US$ 1.00. This means that the currency rises and falls with the fortunes of the U.S. Dollar. So long as the country trades mostly within the U.S. and Caribbean trading area, there may be no need for the XCD to either devalue or up value unless the entire XCD monetary zone is forced to make a change because of overall regional balance-of-payments deficits.

V- International Affairs [8]

The United States has friendly relations with St. Kitts and Nevis, but it has no embassy in the country. Diplomatic relations are maintained through the American Embassy in Barbados and through the St. Kitts and Nevis embassy in Washington D.C. St. Kitts and Nevis in turn is intent in staying friendly with the United States because much of its debt is either bankrolled or guaranteed by Washington.

The country tries to stay in good standing maintains cordial relations with all its trading partners and indeed with most nations in the world. It has the usual memberships in the United Nations, the World Bank and related international organizations, it is also a member of the Caribbean Community and Common Market (CARICOM) and the Organization of eastern Caribbean States (OECS). It receives some assistance through the Caribbean Basin Initiative (CBI) and the United States Agency for International Development (USAID). However, the financial help it is receiving has not been enough to cover its debts.

The focus of attention for St. Kitts and Nevis is similar to that of other east Caribbean islands facing slow growth. It is to establish international connections that will jump start its economic growth and development. The challenge for the country and its neighboring islands is to work closer together through regional organizations like the CARICOM (the Caribbean Community and Common Market). Progress to this end has been slow.

There has been specialized American government assistance to target drug traffickers who have been using the country as a transit point for narcotics from South America to North America and Europe, but any funding in this respect has not significantly trickled down to the domestic economy. There has been evidence of money laundering but not enough to raise international eyebrows.

VI- SWOT Analysis

1- Strengths

As in Anguilla and in most of the eastern Caribbean islands, small size, great weather and tourist friendly populations are strengths in the sense that the island is not a threat to anyone and offers a welcome mat to those seeking a laid-back vacation retreat. St. Kitts and Nevis is a popular tourist destination and has the skilled labor to manage and operate the industry.

2- Weaknesses

A scarcity of natural resources, except for those that draw tourists, are weaknesses that threaten hindering the country's capacity to develop large economy of scale industries that can quickly raise incomes from wages and salaries. Tourism has excellent potential for expansion but it lacks the investment, infrastructure and facilities for that potential to bear fruit.

3- Opportunities

An alternative approach, using the education, experience and know-how of the labor force as an opportunity, could be to supplement the tourism industry with higher-value, high paying activities that occupy niche markets including more outsource activities that help multinational companies service their larger markets. The investments required for these enterprises might need to be of a longer term nature, but the real returns to investors and workers might be much greater.

What will be needed to move St. Kitts and Nevis faster in this direction is a higher level of international cooperation through the existing regional associations like CARICOM. It may eventually be necessary for individual nations within the group to agree to specialize in just one or two high technology industries servicing larger foreign markets that do not compete against their association partners. If, for example, St. Kitts and Nevis decides to concentrate on electronics, Dominica could turn to wearing apparel, St. Lucia could focus on telecommunications, Grenada could try exotic processed foods and St. Vincent and the Grenadines could try rare processed coffees, spices and eco-tourism.

4- Threats

Hurricanes are the main physical threats to the country's economic growth. Violent storms have struck St. Kitts and Nevis in the past with devastating consequences. The threat from hurricanes cannot be eliminated, but attention to more stringent construction codes and more sophisticated early warning systems can minimize the havoc wrought by storms and other cataclysmic events like earthquakes and volcanic activity.

G- Summary and conclusions

The background of St. Kitts and Nevis mirrors that of many countries and territories in the West Indies. It bears the scars of a society based on slavery and that leaves little doubt that its past has retarded the nation's growth and that it has had to struggle to survive as a viable society in the world's family of nations. Still, it is a middle income country and the tourism industry has been good for the two islands. But, it needs much more than tourism to advance its economy. Alone, it is too small and too dependent on the outside world to unilaterally shape its own destiny must therefore work with its neighbors to create those synergistic relationships that will accelerate its growth and development.

The World Bank ranks St. Kitts and Nevis as No. 54 in its Human Development Index (HDI) with a rank of 0.821. The country has not ranked by Transparency International's Corruption Index and the World Economic Forum's Competitiveness Index. [10]

Saint Kitts and Nevis

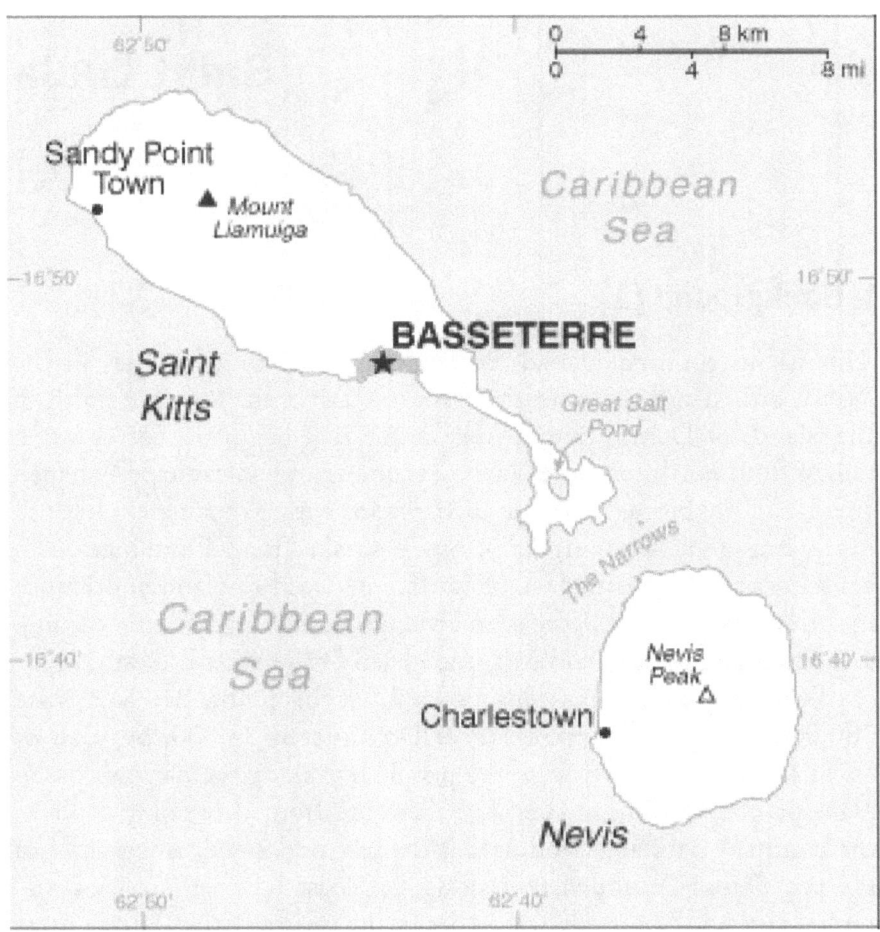

Source: CIA World Fact Book, October 2008 (web accessed, 10/20 08

16

Saint Lucia

I- Background [1]

This island country, named for Saint Lucy of Syracuse, lies in the Windward Islands sector of the Eastern Caribbean. It is due south of the islands of Dominica and Martinique that begin the sector when sailing from north to south. Its mountainous and volcanic pear shaped area is slightly bigger than that of Barbados with 378 square miles (27 miles long and 14 miles wide), but is smaller than Dominica. As a consequence of almost constant warfare between England and France in the 1600's and 1700's, the island changed hands many times, earning it the tongue-in-cheek name of "the Helen of the West Indies." [2]

Demographic comparisons are useful at this point. Barbadians are 280,000 strong. The population of Dominica is 73,000, but that of St. Lucia is 171,000. Most of the people live along the narrow coastal plain on the Caribbean side and therefore from this point of view, the country's habitable land area is densely populated. About half of the population is sandwiched along the coast between Castries, the capital city, and Soufriere, which lies in the shadow of St. Lucia's most illustrious attractions, the two Pitons mountains that can be seen from the sea as twin sentinel peaks silently watching over their domain. [3]

St. Lucia's terrain is more mountainous than any of the other Leeward and Windward islands. Mount Gimie is the tallest mountain in the island and in the region at 3,120 feet and rises from the center of the island from where it can be seen far out at sea. Although there has been no volcanic action of note for many years, the island is geologically active and this has made it a destination for ecology minded travelers. It boasts the world's only drive-in volcano at Soufriere (Sulfur Springs), and its botanical gardens, rain forests and its historical landmarks (Fort Rodney) are international attractions.

Another outstanding feature is the island's largely unspoiled natural features, especially in the vicinity of Marigot Bay which has made it a magnet for wealthy second-homers from North America and Europe. It is said that George Foreman and Mick Jagger have vacation houses near Marigot Bay, but that remains to be substantiated. What is known is that St. Lucia has produced two Nobel laureates: Sir Arthur Lewis (economics) in 1979 and Derek Walcott (literature) in 1992. [4]

The population is mostly of Black African origin (82%). There is a mixed minority (12%), an Indo-Caribbean minority of South Asian origins at 2.5% of the population, a White Anglo/European cohort descended from the European settlers of the past (1%), and small settlements of Lebanese, Syrians and East Asians at 2.5% of the population. English is the official language but a creole mixture of French, Carib and African languages is spoken by most of the people. [5]

The majority religion is Catholicism (70%). Seventh-day Adventists account for 7% of the population and Pentecostals, Anglicans, Evangelicals contribute another 10%. The last 13% breaks down among Rastafarians, Hindus, Moslems and smaller represented religious groups.

The country is officially known as the Commonwealth of St. Lucia and is governed as a constitutional democracy under a limited monarchy. The English crown is the sovereign and head of state, and is represented in St. Lucia by a governor-general. The head of the country's government is a prime minister who is usually selected from the political party that has won the most votes in periodic elections for the House of Assembly's 17 seats. The parliament is actually a bi-cameral legislature consisting of the House of Assembly and a Senate with 11 seats that are appointed. The country is a typical "banana" republic whose economy is based on agriculture led by bananas. While it is moving to diversify into tourism, the wholesale/retail trade, financial services and light manufacturing, much of the labor force, directly and indirectly, works in the agricultural sector in a labor-intensive and low wage environment. St Lucia's economy has stagnated until the last few years and is just now beginning to recover and grow. Life expectancy at birth is 73 years. Adult literacy rate is about 95%, and the average annual per capita GDP is $6,707.00. St. Lucia's GDP Index is 0.702, compared to the U.S. index of 1.000. [6]

II- History [7]

Typical of most of the Caribbean, the Arawak Indians, who had settled the area long before the arrival of Europeans, were marginalized by the Caribs who followed them from Central and South America. By the time Europeans arrived, the Caribs controlled most of the region. They contested the islands against the Europeans until the end of the eighteenth century, suggesting that they had an excellent military organization and a good working knowledge of the sea.

They lacked wind and sail technology but they had sea-going canoes that could hold 100 men that were fast enough to catch a sailing ship. And what they lacked in military hardware they made up with sophisticated skills in the areas of strategy and tactics.

Europeans, beginning with the Spanish, began arriving in the last decade of the 1400's, attempting to gain footholds, only to be repulsed and driven back into the sea. The Dutch landed near what is today called Vieux Fort in 1600 and built a fortification. It had to be abandoned within two years in the face of hostile action by the locals. An English vessel on the way to Guyana in 1605 landed accidentally in St. Lucia and planted a settlement of 67 colonists. Five weeks later the settlement was reduced to 19 colonists through disease and fighting with the Caribs. It is said that the colonists left in the middle of the island for less hostile islands. The French claimed the island in 1635, but the English tried again to build a settlement in 1639. It was destroyed in short order by the Caribs. The French tried again in 1651 from Martinique, and this time, through much bloodshed and killing, their settlements were able to at least survive if not to grow. The English in 1664 challenged the French for control and arrived with 1,000 soldiers. Only 90 men were left at the end of two years, the rest being killed off by disease and by the Caribs who were now allied with the French.

And so life went for the rest of the 1600's, St' Lucia serving mostly as a sacrificial and negotiating pawn between England and France who engrossed in what they thought were bigger wars over more important issues. This all changed when the English and French discovered in 1765 that sugar cane could be mass cultivated on the island. This resulted in two developments that basically changed the dynamics of its political, economic and social culture forever.

The first development was the introduction of indentured English labor followed by the importation of slaves from Africa to work the plantations. This soon assured that with White immigration from Europe and North America dwindling there would be a dramatic change in the ratio of Blacks to non-Blacks.

The second was on-going war with the Carib Indianss. It ended poorly for them by the 1820's when endless confrontation and diseases brought by the Europeans decimated their ranks and reduced them to a handful of survivors who fled to the island's more remote and inhospitable Atlantic side. A few Carib descendants survive to this day.

Slavery was firmly entrenched in St. Lucia when the French Revolution began in 1789. Under French occupation at the time, the island was caught in a tug of war between the Royalists who wanted to preserve slavery and the revolutionaries who wanted to abolish the practice. A guillotine was even brought in from Paris to start executing the Royalists.

However, the English interceded, took over the local government and preserved both the Royalists and their plantation allies and of course the institution of slavery. The French republicans returned in force in 1796 and in alliance with the slaves routed the English, burning Castries and other towns to the ground in the process.

Except for sugar, St. Lucia was never politically or economically important to England or France. The European conflict on the island reflected more a clash of egos over what many considered then a piece of worthless real estate whose upkeep cost much more than its value. Great Britain finally prevailed when in 1815 France traded England St. Lucia for concessions elsewhere. The island remained under the English crown until it earned its full independence in 1979.

An interesting aspect about the slavery issue in St. Lucia is that England outlawed the slave trade throughout the British Empire in 1807 three years after Haiti became the first republic populated largely by former slaves in the Western Hemisphere.

Outlawing the slave trade did not end slavery in St. Lucia. The practice itself endured until 1834 when it was officially abolished by the Empire. But even after slavery ended, former slaves had to agree to an additional four year period of forced labor under the pretext that it was an "apprenticeship" for freedom. Slave revolts in St. Lucia were not widespread occurrences like in Barbados. Hence, St. Lucians did not organize themselves into a political force as did Barbadians. It may also be noted that St. Lucia's early political leaders, many of whom were not educated in Europe or America, did not share the socialist and proletarian leanings experienced by their Barbadian colleagues. A further complication is that the island did not have it own government until well into the last century.

In 1838, the power of government was moved to Barbados, and it 1885, it was moved to Grenada. It was by sheer luck that the island's government was moved back to Castries when a new constitution in 1924 gave St. Lucia limited representative government under the control of England. What was happening in fact was that England was changing from a capitalist to a socialist society and its philosophy was slowly creeping into its offshore possessions.

Universal adult suffrage became law in St. Lucia in 1951 and the practice of ministerial government (a prime minister selected by the majority party) was initiated in 1956. The country joined the West Indies Federation in 1958. The federation lasted until 1962 when its members went their separate ways. St. Lucia opted for the status of "associated state." That gave the country internal self-government in 1967, an arrangement lased until 1979 when St. Lucia became independent and member of the Commonwealth of Nations.

III- Political Environments [8]

The roles played by the United Workers' Party and its leaders, Sir John George Melvin Compton and Sir George Frederick Lawrence Charles, in the process of bringing St. Lucia to independence and to its present state of political and economic development cannot be ignored.

John Compton was born in 1925 in St. Vincent and the Grenadines and moved with his family to St. Lucia in 1939. He had no particular political and economic philosophy but he had an in-born love for politics.

After attending the University College of Wales and the London School of Economics, he became an attorney (1951), returned to St. Lucia and started his political career by winning an election for a seat in the new legislature in 1954. He joined the Saint Lucia Labor Party (SLP) in 1956, whose leader was the charismatic George Charles, and participated in the workers' sugar strike in 1957. His arrest during the strike secured his national popularity and he became Minister of Trade and Production and his party's deputy leader in 1958. He was also active in promoting workers' interests in those areas that were shifting to bananas, the country's new cash crop. This focus was interrupted when George Charles, as party leader, became the country's chief minister in 1960 and appointed Compton to the post of minister of trade and industry.

George Charles, in contrast to John Compton, was older, being born in St. Lucia in 1916 (he died in 2004). Educated at St. Mary's College, he left for Aruba and worked in the oil industry before returning to St. Lucia to join the trade union movement. He was in a sense the country's socialist conscience, reflecting many of the ideas that were gaining credence in England at the time. He rose steadily in the ranks until 1950 when he and a small group of like-minded labor leaders formed the Saint Lucia Labor Party which from its start became the country's majority party.

England had no fundamental aversion to the goals of George Charles and the SSLP and championed their cause as independence approach with the result that in 1960 Charles found himself in the position of chief minister and the country's head of government. Charles remained as chief minister until the SLP lost power in 1964 to a new political party, the United Workers' Party (UWP) led by none other than John Compton. The SLP assumed the role of opposition party for much of the time since 1964 on through to the current decade.

The formation of the UWP was a reaction to John Compton's falling out with his old mentor, George Charles, when it became obvious that the power and influence of the SLP was slipping. Compton left the party after winning re-election to the legislature in 1961 and formed the National Labor Movement that, with the People's Progressive Party, morphed into the UWP and wrested power away from the SLP in 1964. John Compton became the chief minister until the country became independent in 1979 when his title changed to prime minister.

The SLP won the elections in 1979 but lost again to the UWP in 1982 which remained in power until 1997 when the SLP won 16 of 17 seats in the legislature. The SLP won again in 2001 but lost to the UWP, led by John Compton, in 2006.

George Charles was 88 years old when he died in 2004 and had been eclipsed from political life for years. John Compton was 81 years old when he once again assumed the prime minister's post in 2006.

Compton's popular support came from the sugar-cane workers who he had organized a half century earlier and his win for a seat to represent voters in Micoud North was quite decisive if not totally overwhelming (he won the seat by 1,000 votes). He was so popular that his supporters indicated that they needed only his name and not his participation to win. He himself is supposed to have bragged that he was not running for the Olympics but for the leadership of the nation.

However, all good things must come to an end, and so it was to be with John Compton. He was temporarily incapacitated by a stroke in May, 2007. He recovered to resume his role as prime minister but suffered another setback during the summer. He died quietly in his sleep on September 7, 2007. He was 83 years old. Stephenson King, the acting prime minister, promptly declared a two-week mourning period.

A special election in Micoud North in November of that year was easily won by John Compton's daughter, Janine Compton-Rambally, and the UWP still remains in power and Stephenson King is officially the prime minister.

The current governor-general is Pearlette Louisy who represents Queen Elizabeth II of England as Head of State. The legislature has en elected Assembly of 17 seats and an 11 seat Senate whose members are selected by the governor-general in consultation with the prime minister and other political leaders. The Assembly and Senate represent the eleven districts into which St. Lucia is divided: Anse la Raye,

Canaries, Castries, Choiseul, Dennery, Forest, Gros Islet, Laborie, Micoud, Soufriere and Vieux Fort.

The judiciary is independent with a number of district courts and one high court from which appeals may be taken to the Eastern Caribbean Court of Appeals. Final appeals, if the process goes that far, may be argued before the Privy Council's Judicial Committee in London. It is difficult to find a deep philosophical division between the SLP and UWP. They are both basically labor oriented with a socialist bent. It is probably correct to state that the UWP is slightly more labor-friendly and that the SLP today is more pro-business.

IV- Economic Environments [9]

About one third of the country's 172,000 people live in and around Castries, the capital city that rises gently from a coastal plain into lush, green hills dotted with elegant homes inter dispersed with simpler dwellings housing those who obviously toil for a living. If superficial appearances mean anything, the city's downtown thoroughfare reflects this duality of economic fortune.

The city's architecture is post-1948, the year most of the downtown area was destroyed by fire. Therefore, much of its colonial charm is gone, replaced by newer neighborhoods that are nevertheless neat, breezy and pleasant to behold. Government agencies and many businesses are housed in modern, low lying buildings on wide streets landscaped with flowering shrubs and shade palms within sight of open street markets and narrow streets lined with simple, clapboard stores and living quarters.

Castries is the country's busiest harbor and is a half hour walk to the center of the city and its major open air markets, office buildings, businesses and urban residential areas.

Retail outlets ranging from very expensive and chic to the less extravagant discount outlets are well in evidence, and restaurants and eateries for every taste are everywhere. A testament to the changing times in St' Lucia is a Home Depot outlet that opened its doors on the road to Rodney Bay a few years ago.

The World Bank classifies St. Lucia as a middle income country, neither rich nor poor. Despite the government's left of center orientation, the average wage rate for labor is not higher than $100.00

weekly and about 30% of the labor force works for the civil service. But it is clear that it is an economy in transition. It is trying to change from an agricultural base to one driven by value-adding higher technology enterprises based on the use of skilled, educated labor in production and management that generate higher wages and salaries. The government, to this end, is promoting investments into financial services, light manufacturing and tourism in a move to rapidly diversify away from sugar and bananas. Indeed, it is the saga of those two commodities that deserves attention.

Sugar was the island's main source of income from the 1700's to the 1900's. Demand for sugar eased in the first half of the twentieth century and it was replaced by bananas as the cash crop of choice. But success was relatively short lived. The problem was that, as in the case of sugar and most plantation products, bananas are commodities whose market value can change rapidly with changing circumstances. In the 1960's over 70% of export earnings came from bananas shipped to the United Kingdom. This was fine until England joined the European Union (EU) in 1973 and began adhering to it rules of what could or could not be imported. So long as the EU offered its former colonies free and open access to its markets, St' Lucia's banana exports were safe. However, overall European demand for bananas never grew and sometimes declined as tastes changed. The death knell came in 2006, not unexpectedly, when the EU specifically declared that preferential access to its markets for bananas from the Windward Islands would be ended.

The current situation is unclear. An effort to diversify agriculture into other crops like mangos and avocados is showing signs of commercial success, but here again there are the problems of unrelenting international competition and changing demand. St. Lucia is also trying the light manufacturing route. However, this type of industry is mainly an out-source occupation relying on contracts from wealthier post-industrial societies that are phasing out some of their own manufacturing operations. It prospers so long as business models do not change with the foreign primary contractors.

On a more positive note, infrastructure improvement has encouraged Hess Oil to build a tank farm and transshipment terminal. This has been the major foreign investment to date. Funding from the Caribbean Development Bank is also helping the country's airport expansion program.

The government has been promoting tourism and financial services since the 1990's. The hope is that with the growth of tourism there will be more demand for financial services. The country has had a checkered record of success and failure in both industries. Tourist receipts rose annually, despite the ravages of several hurricanes, until September 11, 2001. The terrorist attacks coupled with an economic downturn slowed tourist arrivals to a trickle and several major hotels either closed down or went bankrupt.

It is claimed that in 2007 St. Lucia welcomed about 900,000 visitors and expects this number to rise to about 1,000,000 in 2008. It must be noted in this connection that the country does not have enough capacity to host so many people on an overnight basis. Most of the tourist arrivals were and are day trippers from the many cruise ships who include St. Lucia in their itineraries.

A slow economy has generated a 20% unemployment rate. That has helped keep the annual domestic inflation rate under 2%. The overall economy has been growing at the average annual rate of 3% since 2005. It is still to be seen how changes in the economies of North America and Europe will impact the country in the near future.

Neither has St. Lucia done well in its international transactions. It maintains a huge merchandise trade deficit, importing about $5.00 for every $1.00 it exports. Its major export customers by order of importance are: France, the United States, China, England and Brazil. Its import partners by order of importance are: the United States, Trinidad and Tobago, Netherlands, Venezuela, Finland, England and France. The country currency is the East Caribbean Dollar which is pegged to the U.S. Dollar at EC$2.700 per US$1.00. This means that if the US dollar rises or falls, the EC dollar will do the same.

V- International Affairs [10]

St. Lucia is intent on maintaining good relations with all the countries with which it does business. Aside from its memberships in the United Nations, the World Bank and related international organizations, it is also a member of the Caribbean Community and

Common Market (CARICOM) and the Organization of eastern Caribbean States (OECS).

The country is a recipient of American assistance through the Caribbean Basin Initiative (CBI) and the United States Agency for International Development (USAID). However, it must be stressed that St. Lucia has not received as much assistance as it could have used and is deeply in debt.

The main goal of St. Lucia's international relations is to establish connections that will jump start its economic growth and development. Progress in this pursuit has been slow to materialize.

American government assistance has not been free. The United States has been waging a war on illegal drugs for years and has enlisted St. Lucia's support for drug trafficking and marijuana cultivation control. St. Lucia is one of many transit points in the Eastern Caribbean supply line in the flow of narcotics from South America to North America and Europe and the United States is interested in breaking the supply chain.

VI- SWOT ANALYSIS

1- Strengths.

St. Lucia's strength is its brand of constitutional democracy that has endeavored to establish orderly and representative government under a rule of law. It is also blessed with warm weather that makes it attractive to tourists seeking a tropical vacation. It also has an abundant flora resource base that can be developed into a niche market for toiletries, cosmetics and specialty foods.

2- Weaknesses.

Like all the other countries in the Eastern Caribbean, St. Lucia is too small to contend as a major player in world affairs and global enterprise unless it discovers a scarce and high-demand resource or makes a technological breakthrough with similar results. It may be an active member of many regional and international organizations, but without any real bargaining chips to date, it will be difficult to reap significant and lasting benefits from those long standing associations. A poorly developed internal infrastructure and a relatively weak communications and transportation system increase the difficulties of attracting the investment resources needed for achieving sustained economic growth.

3- Opportunities.

Tourism offers the greatest immediate opportunity for accelerating the country's economic growth and reducing its high unemployment rate. St. Lucia already receives many visitors annually who arrive on cruise ships. While this is noteworthy, the cruise ship tourists spend less than a day on average on land, denying the economy the revenues it would normally receive from overnight visitors. Increasing room capacity should help and interesting opportunities do exist. These will require large scale investments in hotel construction and all related tourism related services. What will also be needed is an expansion of airport facilities and a dramatic increase in the number of direct, non-stop flights from Europe and North America.

4- Threats.

St. Lucia has no external enemies except for the occasional hurricane. The only threat it faces is its internal divisiveness in terms of a lack of focus on achieving economic growth objectives. There is to date scant evidence of concerted policies and programs by the government designed to turn the country's environment from a economic backwater into a more dynamic and progressive society. This economic retardation is seen here as a significant threat to the small nation's continued independence.

VII- Summary and Conclusions

It can be concluded that although St. Lucia has achieved political independence, it has yet to make real economic progress to the extent of Barbados. Its reliance on agriculture and public sector services and its lagging infrastructure renders it uncompetitive in world markets. Investments in private sector industries that pay higher wages and add value to the economy are needed. Concentration on low wage, labor intensive enterprises such as agriculture and small scale manufacturing has done little to improve individual worth and material well being. Hence, St. Lucia remains dependent on foreign economic assistance and is trapped in a neo-colonial time warp.

The World Economic Forum has no data for St. Lucia in its annually published survey of global competitiveness rankings and scores for reporting countries. But, Transparency International's Corruption Perceptions Index ranks it as #72 out of 179 countries with a score of 6.8. [11] The World Bank's Human Development Index ranks it as #72 out of 177 countries with a score of 0.795. [12]

Saint Lucia

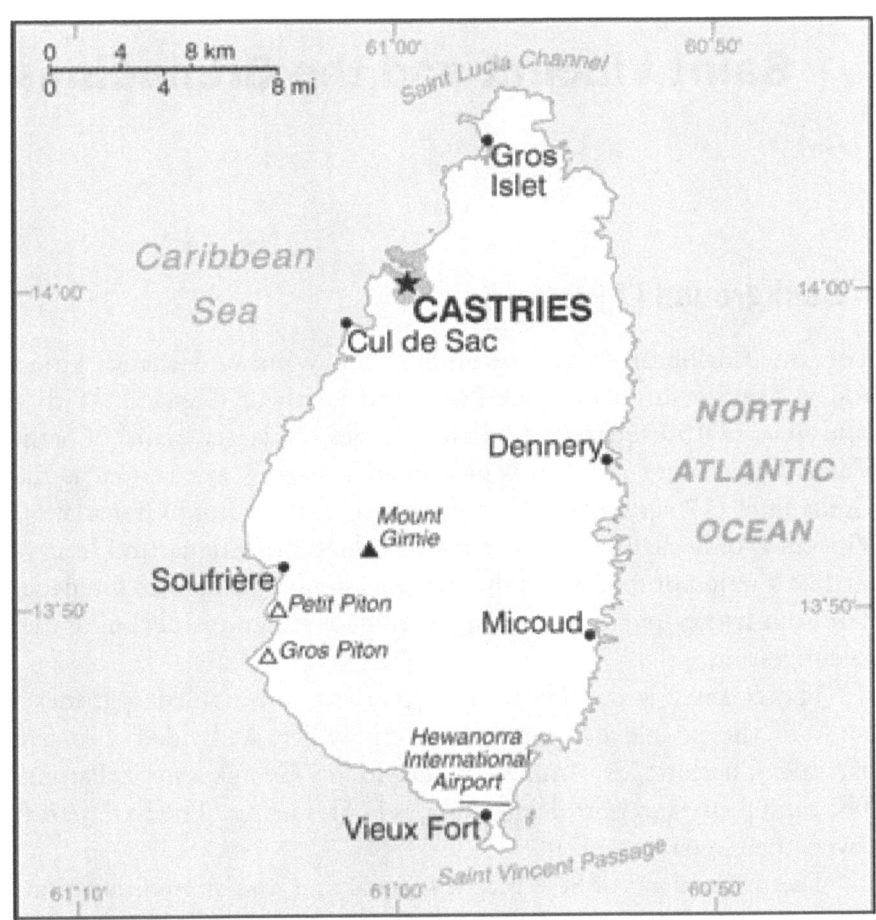

Source: CIA World Fact Book, October, 2008 (web accessed 10/23/08)

17

Saint Vincent and the Grenadines

I- Background [1]

This east Caribbean island nation is in the Windward Islands group and is directly south of Saint Lucia and north of Grenada. With a land mass of 150 square miles that includes the larger island of Saint Vincent and about two-thirds of a small string of cays known as the Grenadines (17 square miles in all) that separate it from Grenada, St. Vincent is only slightly smaller than the island of Antigua, and its cays are like a string of tiny pearls that serve as stepping stones to Grenada. The country's population is 118,000 as of 2009 and is declining due to emigration.

The country is divided into six political units called "parishes." Most of the people live on St. Vincent which is divided into five parishes: Charlotte, St. Andrew, St. David, St. George and St. Patrick. The capital city and port, Kingstown, is in St. George. The sixth parish covers the Grenadines. [2]

The main island of St. Vincent is attracting tourist attention since opening its new international airline facility with a mile long runway that can accept long distance flights.

The island of Bequia, the largest one in the Grenadines, lies directly one hour south of St. Vincent by ferry. It is a popular destination for day trippers from Kingstown and also attracts many overnight and multi-night tourists who frequent its many hotels and inns. It is, like St. Vincent, a favorite with mariners. Its anchorages attract an eclectic assortment of international travelers, hikers, sailing families and luxury yachts.

Mustique, south of Bequia, is a private island upon which exclusive villas are hidden in verdant hillsides. Its beaches and anchorages are sought after by the jet and yachting set.

Canouan is the next cay south of Mustique. Its 1200 residents are rapidly giving up subsistence farming in favor of catering to the growing influx of tourists who now take advantage of new paved roads and daily flights from Puerto Rico and Barbados that bring wealthy tourists to the new Raffles resort. The island boasts a world class golf course and casino (Trump investments) and new investments are planned.

Mayreau is the smallest Grenadine and has less than 200 inhabitants, a small village with two inns and no bank. It has no water except for rain captured in barrels.

Directly to its south is Union Island, a hilly cay capped by Mt. Parnasus. Its main town, Clifton, has a few shops, restaurants, guesthouses and a small, busy airport and yachting center that is now making it a local transportation for the southern Grenadines. Within sight of Union island is Prune Island. It was once a mosquito infested mangrove swamp but has been converted into Palm island with a high-end resort hotel.

Peter St. Vincent is also a reclaimed mangrove swamp island that is now home to a number of private luxury cottages.

Last but not least are the uninhabited Tobago cays. They are south of Canouan and east of Mayreau. They are surrounded by a reef and boast beautiful palm shaded beaches.

Saint Vincent is volcanic and mostly mountainous. The La Sourfriere volcano is active and rises to a height of over 3,600 feet on the north central part of the island. It erupted in 1902, killing 2,000 people. It exploded again in 1979. There were no fatalities but many thousands had to be temporarily evacuated and extensive damage occurred.

The country was also battered by hurricanes in 1980, 1987, 1998 and 1999, and much of the commercial banana and coconut crops were destroyed. This combination of storm and volcanic action makes the country geologically unstable and its future unpredictable.

Tourism is a growing up and coming industry but the economy is still dominated by its agricultural sector in which bananas and coconuts are the main cash crops.

The population is 65% Black, 20% mixed, 6% East Indian, 2% Carib Amerindian, and 7% so-called "Other" comprising Portuguese, Pakistani, Syrian and Chinese. The major religious groups are Anglican (47%), Methodist (28%), Hindu (13%), Islam (6%), other Protestant denominations and Seventh Day Adventists (6%). The official language is English but a French patois is also spoken along with a number of other languages. The literacy rate is high at 96%. Longevity is 73 years and the average annual per capita GDP is about $8,000. [3]

II- Historical Environments [4]

As in the case of many of the east Caribbean islands, the Carib Indians had reached and settled Saint Lucia several centuries ahead of the Europeans. In Saint Lucia in particular, they had established a stronghold and successfully prevented until well into the 1700's, more than two centuries after Christopher Columbus embarked on his first voyage across the Atlantic.

Indeed, the first non-Amerindians in the islands part of Saint Lucia and the Grenadines were not Europeans but African Blacks. Little is known as to how and when they arrived. It has been suggested that they could have been runaway slaves from other islands or that they were survivors of a shipwrecked or grounded slave ship. What is known is that they began drifting into the area in the mid-1600's and intermarried with the Caribs over the next few generations. Their offspring were eventually given the name Garifuna or Black Caribs. (In Jamaica, escaped slaves who fled into the country's interior intermarried with the remnants of a Carib population, and their progeny were later called Maroons).

The Black Caribs were a major force in resisting European incursions throughout the 1700's, proving to be a more formidable foe than the original Caribs. Their political and military champion was a Black Carib named Joeseph Chatoyer. He led the Caribs and Black Caribs, with the support of the Franch, to war against the English and French in 1772 in the First Carib War. The Europeans lost and were forced to sign a treaty with the indigenous population. It was, interestingly, the first treaty signed by the English with a local people.

It was probably also the first treaty of that kind to be broken by the English, paving the way for the Second Carib War in which Chatoyer was killed. The war continued after his death, but the French turned against their former Carib allies and guaranteed their final defeat. Joseph Chatoyer is today a national hero in Saint Vincent and the Grenadines, and a monument on Dorsetshire Hill where he died commemorates his life. When the Caribs were subdued 1796, at least five thousand were forcibly deported to the island of Roatan off Central America.

However, it was the French who, arriving in 1719, were the first Europeans to establish a lasting presence in Saint Vincent. They converted the land into a plantation economy with Black slaves imported from Africa and grew coffee, cotton, sugar and tobacco, cash crops that were the country's staple until well into the 1900's. France surrendered Saint Vincent to the English in 1763, but it was ceded back in 1779 only to be handed over to England, this time for good, in 1783. With the abolishment of slavery in 1834, a drastic labor shortage appeared and indentured labor was brought in from Madeira and India.

The labor shortage changed into a labor surplus almost overnight when agricultural commodity prices crumbled in the mid 1800's, impoverishing most of the islands' non-White populations. This also made the colony costly for England to maintain, a situation it faced in much of its Caribbean possessions in that period. A representative assembly with powers of recommendation was approved by England as early as 1776, but it was not until 1925 that a legislative council with law-making powers was allowed. Universal suffrage was finally approved by England in 1951.

Saint Vincent and the Grenadines joined the short-lived West Indies Federati upon its inception in 1958 up to its collapse in 1962. It was re-constituted as an :associated state" with control over its domestic affairs in 1969 and became totally independent in 1979 under the leadership of Milton Cato.

It is today a parliamentary democracy within the Commonwealth of Nations with a head of state (Queen Elizabeth II) and a head of government (Prime Minister, Dr. Ralph Gonsalves).

III- Political Environments [5]

Politics in the country is dominated by two political parties, the Unity Labor Party (ULP) and the New Democratic Party (NDP). The incumbent party as of early 2008 was the ULP. The head of state is represented by a governor-general appointed by the British crown. The head of government is usually the leader of the majority party in power, with that power being shared by a cabinet whose membership is drawn from both parties. The legislature is unicameral (one chamber) that combines a lower house (House of Assembly of 15 elected members) with a 6- member appointed Senate. Government operations are centralized (some have called it statist) with no local self-government in the six parishes that are considered political subdivisions for election purposes. For example, the senators each represent one of the parishes. The Judicial process runs through district courts with appeals to a Caribbean Supreme Court (that has a High Court and Court of Appeals) and then on for a final appeal to the Privy Council in London. local supreme court system

The first political party of note in Saint Vincent and the Grenadines was the People's Political Party (PPP) founded by Ebenezer Joshua in 1952. It began with a strong labor orientation and played an important role in the development of national policy in the few years prior to total independence. It was the majority party until 1966 when it began to lose support with the rise of a middle class and more business oriented society. Defeated decisively in the 1979 elections, it quickly sank into oblivion and was dissolved in 1984.

The second party of note was the St. Vincent Labor Party (SVLP) under Milton Cato's leadership. It ran on a pro-business, pro- U.S., pro-Western, pro- law-and-order and anti-communist ticket and was influential in shaping national policy for twenty years from the mid-1960's to the mid-1980's. The SVLP led the country to independence and won the first post-independence election in 1979.

But by 1984, the electorate had enough of the SVLP. Many thought it had adopted an anti-labor attitude stemming from a distrust of individual rights, social welfare concepts and a laissaiz-faire society free of intrusive government. This growing opposition to the sometimes high handed and arbitrary policies of SVLP easily swept James Mitchell's New Democratic Party (NDP) to power in 1984.

The NDP was able to retain power until 2001 when the ULP won 12 of the 15 seats in the legislature. It has clung to power until this printing, keeping those 12 seats in the 2005 elections.

IV- Economic Environments [6]

Today, 2008, St. Vincent and the Grenadines continues to employ over 60% of its labor force in banana production. In addition, bananas contribute to over 50% of the country's exports and are therefore a major source of foreign currency earnings. This reliance on a single commodity utilizing low cost, unskilled wage labor and for which international demand fluctuates, , leaves the land in a state of economic retardation relative to other countries who have taken steps to diversify into more technology-intensive activities.

Diversification has recently become the focus of public and private sector policy. The line of weakest resistance is seen as tourism and the government has made its promotion central to economic policy, and the new airport is seen as a stepping stone in that direction. It has at the very least led to the construction of new resort hotels, and additional cruise ship and ferry berths are bringing thousands of new visitors each year.

The country hosted more than 160,000 travelers who did at least a single overnight in 2004. This number doubled by 2007 and is expected to keep growing once the current recession ends. Tourism has become the major source foreign currency source, generates more income in foreign exchange than bananas. Of course, cruise ship passengers are day-trippers who do not spend as much on land as do tourists who remain for longer periods of time, but cruise ships do pay substantial berthing charges that stay in the country as a contribution to the economy.

Despite the country being in the Caribbean Community Common Market (CARICOM) and the CARICOM Single Market and Economy (CSME) it has gained more from its participation in the Caribbean Basin Initiative (CBI) sponsored and funded by the United States. Its classification by the United States as a "developing" or "lower middle income country" allows it to ship its output free of import taxes to the U.S. However, the U.S. accounted for slightly less than 10% of its exports in 2005. It is believed that this had not changed significantly by 2008.

In terms of major export markets, the European Community today accounts for 27% of the country's export shipments. Barbados, Trinidad and Tobago and St. Lucia account for another 12% each. However, in terms of major suppliers, the country imports 34% of its needs from the United States, 24% from Trinidad and Tobago, 15% from the European Union, 4% from Japan and 4% from Barbados.

St. Vincent and the Grenadines is a member of the Eastern Caribbean Currency Union (ECCU) and subscribes to the East Caribbean Dollar (XCD) which is issued by the East Caribbean Central Bank (SCCB). It is pegged to the U.S. Dollar at 2.7 EC$ to US$1.00.

The problem is that the country sustains an on-going merchandise trade deficit with the United States and the world. Its currency peg can therefore only be maintained so long as its overall balance-of-payments are in equilibrium. St. Vincent has benefited from foreign services (tourism) and investment inflows in recent years but not enough to offset all the deficits caused from its merchandise trade imbalance. This has raised the country's debt to a level making it difficult for the government to fight the sticky 20% unemployment rate with public sector financed projects.

V- International Environments [7]

It is important for Saint Vincent and the Grenadines to maintain good relations with the United States and makes strong efforts to have close ties to Washington. It is therefore a member of the Organization of American States (OAS) and the Association of Caribbean States (ACS). These associations, like the CBI tend to reflect American interests in Latin America, the Caribbean and the world.

The country belongs to the United Nations, the World Bank, the International Monetary Fund and the World Trade Organization where it tries more often than not to support the views of the United States. This support has been reciprocal. Washington has provided it with generous assistance through the Peace Corp, the CBI and U.S. AID (U.S. Agency for International Development). The U.S. also actively funds a number of humanitarian programs relating to education, healthcare and disaster relief.

VI- SWOT Analysis

1- Strengths

As in St. Kitts and Nevis or in Anguilla and in most of the eastern Caribbean islands, small size, great weather and friendly populations are strengths in the sense that tourists are attracted to such environments which for Saint Vincent and the Grenadines can help jumpstart its economy. The country is becoming a popular destination for vacationers and is going to great lengths to expand its hospitality industry.

2- Weaknesses

The country's natural resources, fertile soil and rich forest land are strengths translating into weaknesses. Traditionally, these resources have served to attract low cost, unskilled and semi-skilled workers to labor-intensive occupations at a great profit to landowners. Perpetuating this weakness is the country's relatively large population which makes it all the more difficult to rapidly convert a low wage society into higher salaried workers.

Another weakness is the inadequacy of domestic savings and the lack of international financing for investments and infrastructure. This situation hampers the introduction of large economy of scale industries catering to foreign markets that can quickly raise local incomes through higher wages and salaries. Tourism has excellent potential for expansion but it needs more investment, infrastructure and facilities for its potential to bear fruit.

3- Opportunities

Expansion into light manufacturing enterprises is an area of interest increasingly being examined by the government. The increase in tourism has generated greater demand for new hotel construction, and that in turn has created a boom in the construction industry which has raised demand for construction equipment and supplies. The heavy machines are imported, of course, but much of the smaller equipment and many of the supplies can be produced locally as some already are.

Diversification into value-adding industries begets economic growth and development. Investments and investment financing are important here, but the availability of skilled human resources is more important.

Greater cooperation with existing regional associations like CARICOM will give small island nations like St. Vincent and its neighbors an opportunity to specialize in economies of scale without necessarily competing against each other. This idea has been broached in the chapter on St. Kitts and Nevis, but it has not been seriously considered by CARICOM or the ACS.

4- Threats

Hurricanes, storms, earthquakes and volcanic eruptions are real threats and obstacles to sustained economic growth. These have repeatedly struck St. Vincent and the Grenadines with destruction that has proven costly and time consuming to repair. The problem is that these natural calamities occur so frequently that the country often has insufficient time to recover before the next catastrophe strikes. While these natural events are unpreventable, better forecasting, stricter construction codes and better early warning systems can reduce damage and minimize loss of life.

VII- Summary and conclusions

Saint Vincent and the Grenadines is an island nation eager to shed its image as a banana republic and in this context is typical of many Caribbean countries. It has, like most of its neighbors, developed viable and lasting institutions of constitutional democracy. That, to many policy makers, is a positive trait when considering the sociopolitical infrastructure thought necessary for sustaining long term economic growth and development.

Democracy alone seems to be no panacea for growth, although there is no evidence that it has a stunting effect either. Nor does a slave background appear to have a long term negative impact. There are Caribbean countries whose economies have surged and those which have not. The descendents of former slaves are well in control of their countries and have done as well as any group of politicians anywhere in the world. St. Vincent is a survivor nation. It survived as an agricultural society and it is beginning to thrive with tourism. It will probably thrive more by spreading to financial services and light manufacturing that normally support tourism and international investments.

The World Bank ranks St. Vincent as No. 93 in its Human Development Index (HDI) with a score of 0.761 as a medium income country. [8] The country is ranked No. 30 in Transparency International's Corruption Index with a score of 6.1. [9] It has not yet been rated by the World Economic Forum's Competitiveness Index.

Saint Vincent and the Grenadines

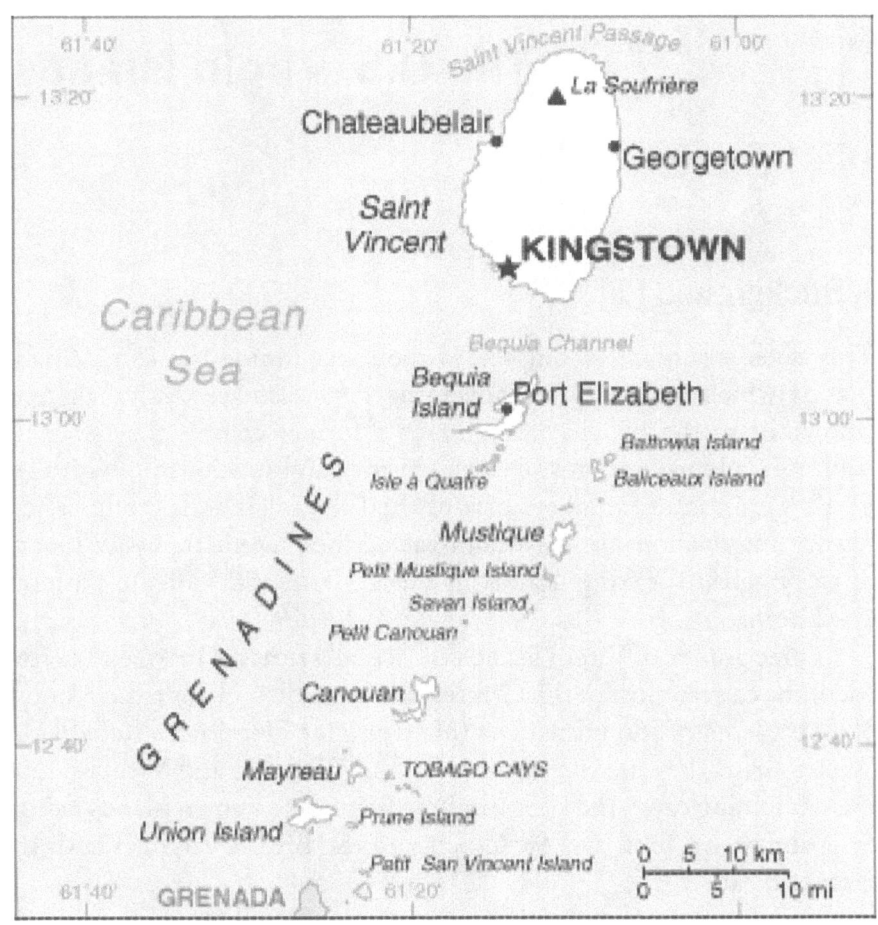

Source: CIA World Fact Book, October, 2008 (web accessed 10/23/08

18

The U.S. Virgin Islands

I- Background [1]

This book would be incomplete without examining the U.S. Virgin Islands which are today self-governing dependencies. Although not connected to the United Kingdom as a former colony, they share a common colonial and post colonial history and relationship with the U. K. Virgin Islands and are part of the Leeward Islands group. That history and relationship has also impacted their interaction with many of the English speaking islands in the Lesser Antilles of the Eastern Caribbean.

Three groups of Virgin Islands are actually situated between Puerto Rico, the easternmost of the Greater Antilles which include the islands of Cuba, Jamaica and Hispaniola (Haiti and the Dominican Republic). West to east, they are the Spanish Virgins (Culebra and Vieques and their adjoining cays), the U.S. Virgins (their better known islands being St. Thomas, St. John and St. Croix) and the British Virgin Islands as discussed earlier.

The Spanish Virgins, however interesting they are, are not reviewed in this book here since, culturally, economically politically and linguistically, they are joined closer to the fortunes of Puerto Rico and the United States than to those of the English speaking Eastern Caribbean. The same might have been said of the U.S. Virgins. The difference is that some politically islanders are beginning to see the future of their society linked closer to the economic and political evolution of their English speaking neighbors in the Leeward and Windward island group than to America. This is a situation that will need closer monitoring by the United States if it plans to keep control in the region.

Three islands are generally fixed in the popular mind: Saint Thomas, Saint John and Saint Croix. Water Island, well known to locals but not to tourists, is a much smaller island that seems to be part of the St. Thomas mainland to the north but is separated from its larger neighbor by a narrow channel. Its bluffs overlook Frenchman's Bay from the west and protect all shipping using the bay to access or leave the harbor of Charlotte Amalie, the town being the capital of St. Thomas. There are many smaller islands or cays that surround the US Virgins, but they have no permanent populations.

The three islands and Water Island have been given interesting nicknames
by locals: Rock City for St. Thomas, Small City for Water Town, Love City for St. John and Twin City for St. Croix. The largest "cities" are Charlotte Amalie in St. Thomas and Christiansted in St Croix. Frederiksted is a small seaport on St Croix's western end. Charlotte Amalie is the administrative and political capital of the USVI's.

The US Virgins are officially organized as an unincorporated territory as of the Revised Organic Act of July 22, 1954. Their total land area is 133.73 square miles, about twice the size of Washington D.C. and faces the Atlantic and Caribbean. Like all of the Caribbean, they are subtropical and lie within the navigational coordinates of 18' North Latitude and 66' West Longitude. The islands are relatively hilly and dry with water being one of the region's scarcer resources. [2]

Their total current population is about 110,000 (as of 2008), and the per capita GDP is less than $14,000. It is estimated that about thirty percent of the people live at or below the poverty level. Half of the population lives in St. Thomas; about 80,000 live in St. Croix and 10,000 reside in St. John. The islands' racial breakdown is: 76% Black, 13% White and 11% mixed and Latino. [3]

The Whites are a mixed group, representing descendants of earlier settlers from England and Denmark and later arrivals from the United States. The growing Hispanic population reflects rising Puerto Rican business activity in the wholesale trades. About 42% of US Virgin islanders are Baptist, 17% are Episcopalian and 34% are Roman Catholic. The rest are Buddhists, Hindus, Jewish, Rastafarians and members of other Asian religions. [4]

US Virgin islanders are American citizens. Although they can vote in all presidential primaries, they do not vote in presidential elections. The local government is in the hands of a locally elected territorial governor whose election has been held every four years since 1970. Between 1946 and 1970, territorial governors were appointed by the U.S. President. The U.S. Navy was responsible for running the islands between 1898 and 1946. [5]

The local economy has not prospered in recent generations. While tourism has replaced agriculture (sugar and rum) as the islands' principal mainstay, it has not generated anticipated results. Full service luxury hotels have dotted the US Virgins for generations, but they have been periodically buffeted by economic reverses in the United States, by hurricanes sweeping through the Caribbean and by competition from the cruise ship industry.

Bad weather, a weak investment infrastructure, inadequate planning and the preference of many tourists to use cruise ships as traveling hotels have helped retard growth and development, leaving much of the economy in a quagmire. With the current downturn in global investment activity, it is difficult to predict when the situation will change.

There is, however, a much deeper problem that afflicts the overall society. The basis for the existence of the USVI's is tourism which since the 1970's has consumed its energy and resources. This too until the 1960's was an issue for stateside sub-tropical economies like Florida where tourism and agriculture dominated had long dominated business activity. Florida changed its direction when public policy decisions were made to expand the breadth of commercial enterprise by diversifying into finance and banking, shipping and transportation, and distribution and warehousing,

The reason for south Florida's success is one of the reasons for stagnation in the USVI's. This chapter will explore some of the other reasons that have led to their current situation. It will also analyze ideas and propositions that might work to accelerate their economic growth and development.

II- Historical Environments

The USVI's appear to have been originally inhabited by Stone Age people known as the Ciboney. They left little evidence except for the assorted flints and stone tools discovered by archeologists in more recent years. How and from where they arrived are arguments still to be settled. If conventional theories are any guide, (namely that repeated overland migrations from Asia were responsible for the first populations in the Western Hemisphere), it might be concluded that the Ciboney people island hopped to the islands on seagoing canoes from the mainland several thousands of years ago. This theory could have validity if it is assumed that they possessed skills needed to build sturdy boats and had some knowledge of offshore navigation. [6]

It is speculated that the Ciboney were eventually displaced by the Arawaks who in turn were overrun by the Caribs from the South American mainland. The Caribs were the major force to be reckoned with by the time Europeans arrived (Christopher Columbus in 1493) and Arawak survivors were largely confined to less fertile islands like the Bahamas and the Turks and Caicos. Indeed, the processes of colonization in the USVI's, beginning with attempts to enslave the local population for the production of sugar, involved a long and bloody confrontation between the Caribs and the Spanish invaders that lasted well into the 1600's. Ultimately, it was probably a combination of war, epidemic diseases, famine and attrition that brought the Arawaks and Caribs to extinction in the USVI's.

The USVI's were fought over by England, Denmark, France, Holland and Spain until 1733 when the Danish West India Company purchased St. Croix from the French and merged it with St. Thomas and St. John, into the Danish West Indies. The Danes devoted their energies to sugar, the only cash crop that was commercially viable in the semi-arid soil. Cheap labor supplied by the indigenous residents died with the Caribs and were replaced with slaves imported directly from Africa or from existing slave markets in neighboring islands. By 1673, the economy of the USVI's was entirely driven by slaves of African origin.

Slavery under European or American masters, an unhappy period in the history of the Western Hemisphere, was especially inhuman in the USVI's under Danish rule. The history of slavery under Danish rule was marked by repeated rebellions with each one being extinguished with ever-increasing violence, repression and cruelty. For some reason, even when slavery was officially banned in most of the Caribbean by 1834, Denmark had no plans to legally abolish slave labor. In 1848, slaves in St. Croix staged an armed revolt and marched on Frederiksted. The local governor, fearing for the lives of its White inhabitants, abolished slavery under duress. It was an act that cost him his career and was condemned by the Danish government with the support of its people. [7]

What has followed from 1848 to 1917, when the United States bought the islands from Denmark, was the development of an Apartheid society, much like it was to be later in the South Africa, where a politically empowered and wealthy minority (less than 20% of the population) managed to dominate the economic and social lives of the vast majority and to keep it in servitude. A change from the Danish to the American flag transferred a legacy of neglect and poverty from Copenhagen to Washington. The government's motivation for acquiring the islands was to protect national security interests in the first World War and their administration was left to the U.S. Navy from 1917 to 1931.

The reason why the U.S. Navy became involved in the administration was logical at the time. With almost no experience as a colonial power beyond the military occupation of lands captured from Spain in the aftermath of the Spanish-American War (1898), it was natural that Washington would leave the USVI's in the hands of the Navy, the reigning military presence in the Caribbean in the early twentieth century. This naval oversight did little to improve local conditions.

American naval personnel at the time, especially its officers, tended to be racist, a sentiment shared with local Scandinavian merchants. Hence, they took a dim view of the ability of the local Black population to handle its own political affairs. However, the Navy did expend considerable resources and energy in modernizing the islands' infrastructure. Finally, under the terms of the Organic Act, the people were granted US citizenship. [8]

In 1946, President Harry S. Truman appointed William H. Hastie as the first Black governor of the USVI's. This also gave Hastie the distinction of being the first African American governor in U.S. history, a fact scarcely noticed on the American mainland, probably because the event occurred offshore. [9]

The new local government was given jurisdiction over the entire USVI's with the exception of Water Island which was kept under the direct control of the Navy. Fifty acres were finally turned over to the territorial authority in 1996, and the remaining land was surrendered for $10.00 in 2005. To this day, the National Park Service owns half of St. John and many of the reefs and cays surrounding the larger islands.

The jet age that began in the early 1960's opened the USVI's and many of the other Caribbean lands, to tourism. A trickle of vacationers and business travelers that marked the flow of visitors in the past turned into a torrent and the islands became a popular destination. Four to five hour flights from the US east coast were becoming an inexpensive routine within reach of middle income families, and investors rushed in to build new hotels, restaurants, shopping centers and combination retirement-vacation homes.

Former sleepy, backwater towns like Charlotte Amalie and Christiansted were transformed into vacation getaways within a decade. It also helped that by the 1960's central air conditioning, or at least window units, had become a standard for most tourist accommodations.

The 1960's and 1970's were perhaps the highpoint of prosperity for the USVI's. There were enough hotel rooms to house visitors of all incomes and hourly flights from Puerto Rico brought same-day tourists to the stores of Charlotte Amalie and Christiansted for duty-free liquor, cigarettes, cameras, jewelry and other luxury goods.

This good fortune lasted until the 1980's when hurricanes alternating with downturns in the economy of the American mainland brought progress to a grinding halt. Hotels and shops shuttered their doors and the number of daily and longer term visitors stagnated. Complicating the climatic and economic situations were the large cruise ships that arrived in increasing numbers from Florida, Puerto Rico and mainland US ports and to compete directly against the local hotel industry.

The USVI's are at a crossroads today. Total independence from the United States is an option being examined by some political leaders, an idea that has been neither encouraged nor discouraged by Washington.

The overall plan of independence would be for the islands to become more closely connected politically to the former English colonies of the Eastern Caribbean. This is a concept that has also been floated periodically in the British Virgin Islands. It never achieved much traction in Road Town and has been more unpopular in Charlotte Amalie.

Tourism alone will probably not solve poverty and economic retardation in the USVI's. But neither will independence despite its emotional attraction as a cure all for economic ills. Without Washington's continuing support, it is difficult to see how the islands would survive as viable political units, just as it is unrealistic to suppose that full independence and national sovereignty would change the basic circumstances surrounding their material wellbeing. Sustaining economic growth in the islands will require the development of globally or at least regionally competitive enterprises and infrastructure that can successfully cope with the forces of nature.

III- Political Environments

The USVI's are legally considered as an "organized incorporated territory of the United States." This means that they fall under the jurisdiction of the US government but are not part of any US state in the federal union. They are granted internal self-government and have some degree of representation in the federal government but their electorate, although it can participate in national primaries, cannot vote in national elections. In the case of the US Virgin islanders, they do have the option to hold referendums on keeping the status quo, voting for full statehood or voting for full independence and full national sovereignty. Total political independence would add another nation to the English speaking family of nations in the eastern Caribbean. [10]

Three political parties are currently prominent and have been active since the first local elections for a governor were held in 1970. These parties are the Democratic Party of the Virgin Islands, the Republican Party of the Virgin Islands and the Independent Citizens Movement. The Democratic Party broadly reflects the center-left philosophy of the stateside Democrats while the local Republicans tend to be more conservative or center-right. It is noteworthy that both parties tend to agree on maintaining the status of the islands as a territory of the United States,

The Independent Citizens Movement is a smaller, more loosely organized party is a testament to their link to stateside Republicans. The party tends to be socialistic in its philosophy and its basic goal is to achieve nationhood for the islands.

The governor of the USVI's, elected to office every four years, is the head of government with responsibility for the islands' administration. The head of state is the Office of Insular Affairs of the United States Department of the Interior which has responsibility over all federal dependencies. Residents of the USVI's are American citizens but do not vote for the president of the US and do not send voting representatives to the US Congress. They do have the right nevertheless to send a delegate to Congress with the right to vote at the congressional subcommittee level. [11]

The USVI's is governed by a unicameral legislature (one house) made up of 15 senators or representatives. St. Croix elects seven senators as does St. Thomas and St' John. One senator (the fifteenth), a resident of St. John, is elected "at-large" by all USVI residents with the right to vote.

The judiciary of the USVI's is independent and consists of three courts, the District, the Superior and Supreme courts. The District Court is charged with hearing cases affecting federal principles of law (eg., interpretation or application of the US Constitution and US laws). The Superior Court is the trial court for local cases which, on appeal, can be heard by the Supreme Court of the USVI's. The President of the United States appoints judges to the District Court while the Governor of the USVI's appoints the judges to the other courts. [12]

The modern political era for the USVI's can be said to have started in 1946 when President Harry S. Truman appointed William H. Hastie as the islands' first Black governor. Before 1946, the administration of the former Danish colony was left to the US Navy until 1931 and since then left to and minor political presidential appointees who were always White. The glaring fact that William Hastie was a stateside African-American and not from the islands was largely irrelevant to the message delivered by Washington that now the USVI's were ready for a measure of self-government by the local, largely non-White population. This was hailed internationally as a giant step by the American government that Blacks in the Virgin Islands, and for that matter, Blacks anywhere in the United States, should be represented at all levels of government. It was also a welcome relief from centuries of slavery followed by almost another century of economic servitude and political subordination, first to a powerful White minority and then to the U.S. Navy that ended with Hastie's appointment. [13]

IV- Economic Environments

T¹he economy of the USVI's has not fared poorly relative to other states in the eastern Caribbean. The issue is that as a political dependency of one of the wealthier nations of the world the expectation was that the islands would stand out as show cases for America's general prosperity. This unfortunately has not been the case. The dependency's per capita GDP is about $14,000. This is about one third of the overall annual per capita GDP of the USA. In terms of the 33 Caribbean states, the USVI's stand 13 from the bottom.

Three transcending reasons exist for their lackadaisical development. The first is the climate. Returning travelers often describe their picture postcard images of bright sunny skies presiding over sandy beaches shaded by palm trees swaying in gentle breezes. These images are correct during the winter months, the peak of the tourist season. The summer months, however, are marked with hurricanes that sweep over the islands often with devastating frequency. All too often, these storms have wiped away all progress made in the interim. [14]

The second reason is the geology of the USVI's. Like many of the smaller Caribbean islands, they are relatively arid despite periods of heavy rainfall. For example, cacti thrive on St. Croix's eastern side while rain forests reign over the rain catching hills on its western half. In general, the soil is hard and shallow and, except for sugar cane, difficult to cultivate. The land tends also to be volcanic in nature. This has not been a problem anywhere in the entire range of Virgin Islands east of Puerto Rico, but it is worthwhile noting that sudden earth tremors in St. Thomas on October 13, 2008, registered 6.1 on the Richter scale. [15]

The third reason, and perhaps the most important, is that in the many years between the abolition of slavery in 1848 and the political emancipation of the Black majority in 1970 most residents were never given an opportunity to own and manage their economic destiny. This lack of empowerment has turned generations of USVI residents into mendicant societies dependent on outside assistance for sustenance.

Four time frames mark the evolution of the islands since their discovery by the Europeans. The first was a subsistence agrarian economy that copied to an extent the way of life led by the Indians and in which output was limited to goods for immediate consumption. This stage lasted until the 1670's when the practice of slavery was institutionalized for the sugar industry.

Slavery ushered in the sugar plantation era in a time of prosperity, at least for the plantation owners and economic allies. This second time frame lasted until the mid 1800's when world sugar prices fell and the importance of a sugar-based plantation oriented society declined.

The third time frame between the mid 1800's and 1970 was a century long period of economic, political and social stagnation. With due credit given to the political empowerment granted to the islands' Black majority, it was the advent of the jet age and air conditioning that finally brought the hope of a greater prosperity to the general population in what can be considered today the fourth time frame in the economic history of the USVI's.

The fourth time frame began in the 1970's and is still to be completed. It is clear that tourism is a major player in the economy and is its most important employer. About 80% of the labor force works directly or indirectly in the tourism industry. About 2.6 million people visited the USVI's in 2006. It has fallen dramatically in 2007 and 2008 because of the economic uncertainties on the mainland. [16]

It is therefore also evident that tourism alone will not lift living standards anywhere close to U.S. mainland levels. More capital/technology intensive enterprises paying higher wages and salaries will be required sooner rather than later. Before the 1990's, most tourists arrived by plane. Today, most tourists arrive on cruise ships that stop for the day and then move on to the next port of call. This has been a boon for port-side shopping facilities, but it has not helped the more inland hotels, shops and restaurants and has not led to a more equal distribution of income in the islands.

Indeed, a pressing issue for the islands is income distribution. With a full third of the population living at or below the poverty line, the more equal distribution of income is a problem requiring immediate attention if only to preserve societal peace and order.

V- International Environments

The USVI's is on the list of non-self-governing territories published by the United Nations. This distinction is shared by four other states in the English speaking eastern Caribbean, namely, the British Virgin Islands, Anguilla, the Cayman Islands and Montserrat. However, while these islands have played active roles in regional organization in the Caribbean and elsewhere in the world, the USVI's, as a United States territory, does not participate except in a guest or spectator capacity in international forums. Nor is it a signatory for the same reason to international treaties. Most of its political leaders seem to have been content to date to leave cross-border issues strictly in the hands of Washington.

A small independence movement exists, but it has not gained any traction or popular support. In 2007, a United Nations committee on decolonization passed a resolution recommending independence for Puerto Rico, including the Spanish Virgin Islands of Culebra and Vieques, The resolution failed to include the USVI's.

VI- SWOT Analysis

The strength of the USVI's in maintaining a viable political and economic existence depends on its continuing close relationship with the United States mainland. Its balmy, sub-tropical weather is an important asset in the highly competitive tourism industry and represents an excellent opportunity for new investments over the long term. The islands' education infrastructure is as good on average as it is in the States and all children of age are enrolled in the K-12 school system. Many who graduate continue their education in the College of the Virgin Islands and in one of the several technical schools in St. Thomas and St. Croix. The long term USVI government investment in education has been successful in creating a knowledgeable and disciplined labor force with skills necessary to undertake work requiring the functional skills to operate a modern economy geared to servicing the administrative needs of larger land-based societies. The islands' location also places them in the ideal position to serve as a center for the warehousing and distribution of goods flowing to and from the Caribbean islands.

The islands' weakness is its apparent lack of success in attracting the flow of investments necessary to assure sustained growth and development to compensate for temporary reverses stemming from periodic bad weather in the Caribbean and economic downturns on the US mainland. The financial infrastructure of the islands is weak and receives only minimal support from Washington. In terms of the overall economy, it is overly dependent on the federal government, and few positive initiatives have been made to make it more self-sufficient and more competitive. A problem contributing to the general weakness of the USVI's is the local government's lack of clout in Washington's corridors of power and its inability to attract major corporate players to the merits of making long term business investments.

There is life beyond tourism for the USVI's and from this point of view the islands present many untapped opportunities for business investments in enterprises needing an offshore base for the sales, financial, administrative, distribution and warehousing tasks which from a cost benefit analysis cannot be as efficiently executed at stateside locations. A petroleum tank farm with limited refining capacity has been in operation on St. Croix's south coast for several decades, generating a significant amount of employment and income for the local population. An emphasis on expanding those existing facilities should be seriously considered.

Two airports, one in St. Thomas and the other in St. Croix that can handle large jet traffic have been in place since the 1960's. Their main use has been to serve the tourism industry and their potential to handle commercial cargo has yet to be fully explored and exploited. Granted, expansion of the airport on St. Thomas, Cyril E. King International Airport on Red Point, may be limited by the surrounding roads and hills and would require a redesign and reengineering of approaches, runways and the surrounding terrain. However, Henry E. Rohlsen Airport on St. Croix's southern coast near the Hess Oil Refinery is on flat land and can more easily be expanded. Allocating greater use of airport space to airborne commercial cargo would make the USVI's attractive to investors interested in creating a commercial distribution and transportation hub in the northern Caribbean. It would also reduce pressure on the overcrowded facilities of San Juan, Miami and Fort Lauderdale and speed up the moving of high value freight from Latin America to the eastern United States.

An evaluation of the islands' seaports should also be made in the same context of turning them into a major ocean transport hub for trade between North and South America. The current global economic lull notwithstanding, there is bound to be a resurgence and great surge in the movement of goods when the recession ends. Of the two major seaports of entry, Frederiksted in St. Croix and Charlotte Amalie in St. Thomas, the latter seems to offer the greatest expansion potential. It has a deep-water harbor as evidenced by the long cruise ship dock adjoining the Havensight Mall. It is able to handle the largest ocean going ships and the site could lend itself to expansion into a full service commercial maritime center and warehousing complex. These are not inexpensive ventures and would require a coordinated combination of public and private investments. It is nevertheless in the author's opinion the only way the USVI's may be able to grow and develop their economy.

Three threats will face the USVI's forever. The first threat, Hurricanes and storms, are part of the sub-tropical Caribbean scenario and greater attention to architectural design and construction engineering to minimize damage are the only solutions. The second threat, earthquakes, is also part of the picture.

Again, the predictability of damaging earth tremors will mostly likely never change, and only better and higher construction standards will help reduce their destructive capacities. The third threat, water scarcity, calls for the use of technologies to make the USVI's water independent.

VII- Summary and Conclusions

The USVI's, as a political dependency and part of the United States is in a strong position to take advantage of that position to rapidly drive forward its economic growth and development. The islands today are governed as a self governing constitutional democracy and much support is given to businesses investing in the territory. What is needed is a vision to see the Virgin Islands as being more than mere sun drenched tourist havens if they are to enjoy the same great diversity of economic enterprise which has brought prosperity to other sub-tropical areas like south Florida following public policy decisions to broaden its base of activities.

The U.S. Virgin Islands

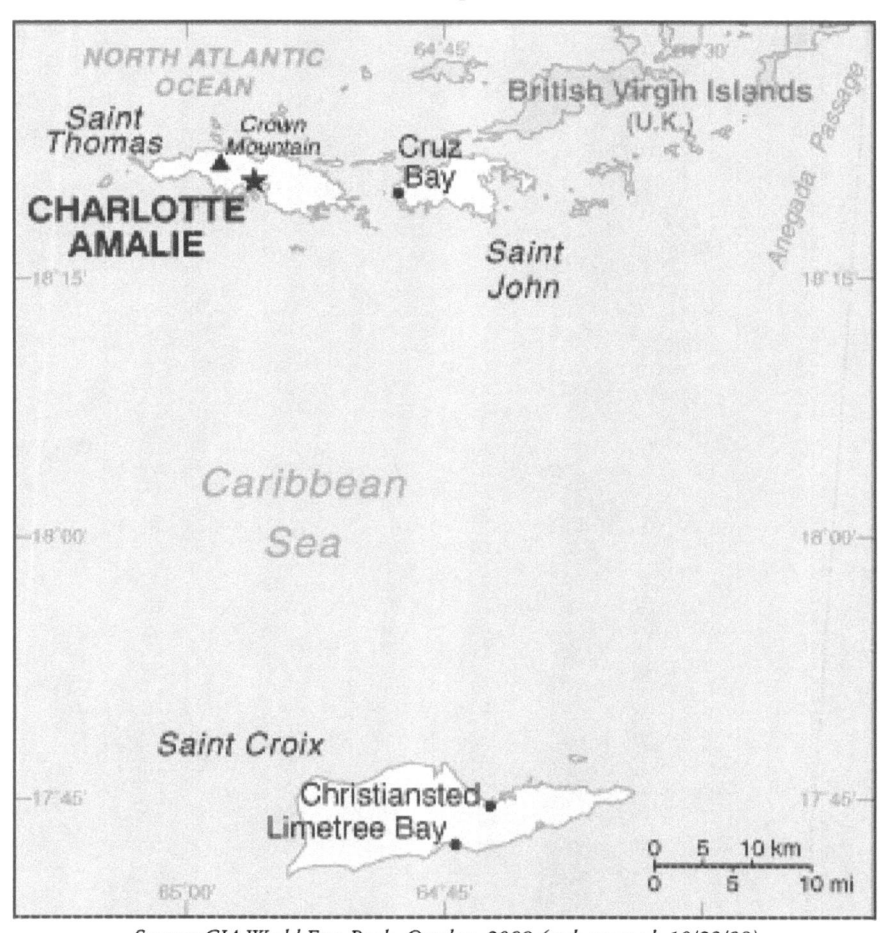

Source: CIA World Fact Book, October, 2008 (web accessed, 10/23/08)

Notes

Chapter 1-

[1] West Indies and Caribbean Yearbook, Caribbean Ltd. Publishers, Toronto, Canada, 1975.
[2] World Development Indicators, 2009, World Bank, Washington DC.
[3] The Last Days of St. Pierre, Ernest Zebrowski, Jr., Rutgers University Press, 2002
[4] Montserrat, Wikipedia

Chapter 2-

[1] Government and Politics in Africa South of the Sahara, Adam, Thomas, Random House, NY, 1959.
[2] Colonial Policy and Practice, Furnivall, Justin, Cambridge University Press, 1956.

Chapter 3-

[1] Words attributed to Cassius Marcellus Clay, Jr., as per Wikiquote, accessed on the Internet, 23 July, 2008.
[2]- Using the United States as a benchmark, its current population is estimated to be about 305 million and its average annual per capita gross domestic product is over $41,000 on a purchasing power parity basis. Source: 2007 World Development Indicators; World Bank, publisher. See: Size of the Economy, Page 16.
[3] See Chapter Three.
[4] "Russia and Venezuela Will Coordinate Energy Policies," New York Times, Page A11, 23 July, 2008.
[5] See Chapter Three.

[6   Martha's Vineyard is 87.48 square miles; Nantucket is 105.3 square miles; Catalina Island is 78.98 square miles. Source: Wikipedia; Internet accessed on 23 July, 2008.

[7] Op cit; 2007 World Development Indicators. See also Chapter Three.

[8   See Anguilla, Chapter 8.

[9] See Grenada, Chapter 13.

[10] See Table I: Map of the Eastern Caribbean.

[11] A statement made in a communication by U.S. Navy Governor Sumner Kittelle to President Warren Harding in 1922 is illuminating. He purportedly stated, "I cannot too strongly urge that there be no change made in the organic law until a full generation has elapsed... and above all the white element must remain in the lead and in... control." This passage is quoted in "Prejudice and Poverty," from America's Virgin Islands, a history of human rights and wrongs, by William Boyer, pages 115-116, Carolina Academic Press, 1983.

[12] See: A Brief History of the Caribbean, Jan Rogozinski, Plume (Penguin Putnam, Inc.) 2000, N.Y.C. ISNB Nos. 0-8160-3811-2 & 0452-28193-8.

[13] As of this printing, Anguilla, Montserrat and the British Virgin Islands remain self-governing dependencies of the United Kingdom.

Chapter 4-

[1] "Grenada," Background Notes, United States Department of Commerce, publication

date: July, 2008; Internet accessed, 24 July, 2008.

[2] See Table II, Map of the Caribbean.

[3] Ibid.

[4] Op cit: Chapter 1, Footnote #2.

[5] See: Individual country chapters.

[6] Ibid

[7] See: Op cit: Background Notes. See also the individual country data published by the Central Intelligence Agency, the CIA World Fact Book, latest Internet access: July, 2008.

[8] Ibid.

[9   World Economic Forum. Internet accessed: 23 July, 2008.

[10]Words attributed to Lynden Pindling at his Independence Day address in Nassau, the Bahamas, on 10, July, 1973.

Chapter 5-

[1] CIA World Fact Book, September, 2009.
[2] World Development Indicators, World Bank, 2009.

Chapter 6-

[1] Race and History, "The Spread of Homo Sapiens," From Raceandhistory.com and, www.ucalgary.ca, Source web accessed on November 5, 2004.
[2] See: "Atlas of World History," Harper Collins/Borders Press, Ann Arbor, Michigan, 1998.
[3 See: Pons, Frank Moya, History of the Caribbean, Markus Wiener Publishers, Princeton NJ, 2007.

Chapter7-

[1] Williams, Eric; Documents of West Indian History, PNM Publishing, Port-of-Spain, Trinidad, 1963. See also: Crew, John A., The Epic of Latin America, Chapter 4, "The New World Meets The Old World, Cross and Sword," Page 65.
[2] Williams, ibid, Page 5.
[3] Williams, ibid, Page 54.
[4] Williams, ibid, Page 8.
[5] Crew, John A., ibid, Page 65.

Chapter 8-

[1] "Anguilla," CIA World Fact Book, October, 2008 (cia.org/library), accessed on 10/25/08.
[2] Ibid.
[3] "Anguilla," Background Notes, U.S. Department of Commerce. org, accessed on 10/25/08.
[4] Op cit., CIA World Fact Book.
[5] Op cit., Background Notes.
[6] A Brief History of the Caribbean, Rogozinski, Jan, Penguin Books, 2000.

[7] Op cit., Background Notes.

[8] Ibid.

[9] Op Cit., CIA World Fact Book.

[10] Ibid.

[11] Ibid.

Chapter 9-

1   "Antigua," CIA World Fact Book, October, 2008 (cia.org/library), accessed on 10/25/08.

2   Ibid.

3   "Antigua," Background Notes, U.S. Department of Commerce. org, accessed on 10/25/08.

4   Op cit., CIA World Fact Book.

5   Op cit., Background Notes.

6   Op cit., CIA World Fact Book.

7   Op cit., Background Notes.

8   Op cit., CIA World Fact Book.

9   Op cit., CIA World Fact Book.

10 "Caribbean Time Bomb," Coram Robert, Wm Morrow & Co., NY 1993. See also, "A Brief History of the Caribbean," Rogozinski, Jan, Penguin Books, 2000.

11 Op cit., CIA World Fact Book.

12 Ibid.

13 Op cit., Background Notes.

14 Ibid.

15 Ibid.

Chapter 10-

[1] "Barbados," CIA World Fact Book, October, 2009 (cia.org/library).*

[2] Ibid.

[3] "Barbados," Background Notes, U.S. Department of Commerce. org,*

[4] Op cit., CIA World Fact Book.

[5] Op cit., Background Notes.

[6] Op cit., CIA World Fact Book.

[7] Op cit., Background Notes.

[8] Op cit., CIA World Fact Book.

[9] Op cit., CIA World Fact Book.

[10]Rogozinski, J., A Brief History of the Caribbean, Penguin Books, 2000. See also: Pons, F.M., History of the Caribbean, Markus Wiener Publishers, Princeton NJ., 2007.

[11]Op cit., CIA World Fact Book.

[12]Human Development Index, World Bank, 2008.

[13]Op cit., Background Notes.

[14] Ibid.

[15]Ibid., See also: Rogozinski and Pons, op cit.

[16]Ibid., See also: Rogozinski and Pons, op cit.

[17]Rogozinski and Pons, op cit.

[18]Op cit., Background Notes.

[19]Op cit., Background Notes.

[20]Op cit., Background Notes.

[21]Op cit., Background Notes

* Data accessed: 10/01/09

Chapter 11-

1 CIA World Fact Book, (cia.org/library) web accessed: August, 2008.

2 See map of the British Virgin Islands.

3 Ibid.

4 CIA World Fact Book, op cit.,

5 Ibid.

6 Ibid.

7 "British Virgin Islands," Wikipedia. Web accessed, August 1, 2008.

8 "British Virgin Islands," pages 76-77, 281, 302-306. A Brief History of the Caribbean, Jan Rogozinski, Penguin Books, 2000; 0-452-28193-8.

9 Ibid. See also: "Slavery in the British Virgin Islands," Wikipedia. Web accessed, 8/2/08.

10 Ibid.

11 A Brief History of the Caribbean, op cit.

12 CIA World Fact Book, op cit.

13 Ibid, See also "Politics of The British Virgin Islands," Wikipedia. Web accessed 8/3/08.
14 Ibid.
15 Ibid.
16 CIA World Fact Book, op cit.
17 Ibid.
18 "Non-Governing Territories Listed by The General Assembly," The United Nations and Decolonization Conference, May, 2008, Web accessed 8/4/08.
19 "Politics of the British Virgin Islands," Wikipedia. Web accessed 8/4/08.
20 CIA World Fact Book, op cit.

Chapter 12-

[1] Documents of West Indian History, Eric Williams, PNM Publishing Co., Port-of-Spain, Trinidad & Tobago, W. I., 1963.
[2] Eastern Caribbean, Lonely Planet Publications, Victoria, Australia, 2001, P.187.
[3] "Dominica," Background Notes, U.S. Department of State. org.
[4] Factmonster.com/ipka/A0004379.html, 11/6/2004.
[5] The story of the Caribs and Arawaks, www.raceandhistory.com/Taino,
[6] "Dominica," CIA World Fact Book (cia.org/library/
[7] "Dominica," Background Notes, op cit.
[8] Ibid; See also: Eastern Caribbean, op cit.; Rogozinski, J., A Brief History of the Caribbean, Penguin Books, 2000; Pons, F. M., History of the Caribbean, Markus Wiener Publishers, Princeton NJ 2007.
[9] Eastern Caribbean, op cit.
[10] Ibid.
[11] "Dominica," Background Notes, op cit., CIA World Fact Book, op cit.
[12] Human Development Index, World Bank, 2009.
[13] Background Notes, op cit.
[14] Ibid
[15] World Economic Form (weforum.org) 2009.
[16] Transparency International, 2009.
[17] Human Development Index, World Bank, 2009.

Chapter 13-

[1] The CIA World Fact Book, October, 2008 (web accessed: August, 2008). [2] "Grenada," Ibid.

[3] "Background Notes," US Dep't of State, (web accessed: August, 2008).

[4] The CIA World Fact Book, op cit.

[5] Op cit.

[6] "Human Development Index, 2007-08," The World Bank.

[7] "Background Notes," op cit. See also Wikipedia web page on Grenada.

[8] "Revolution and Intervention in Grenada," Schoenhals, Kai & Melanson, Richard, Westview Press, 1985.

[9] Ibid.

[10] Ibid.

[11] The CIA World Fact Book, op cit. (See also: Background Notes).

[12] Ibid.

[13] "Revolution and Intervention in Grenada," op cit.

[14] The CIA World Fact Book, op cit.

[15] Ibid.

[16] Ibid.

[17] "Human Development Index, op cit.

[18] "Corruption Index 2007," Transparency International.

[19] "Competitiveness Index, 2007," World Economic Forum.

Chapter 14-

[1] The population of Montserrat before the volcano eruption was 13,000; it has since fallen to 4,500.

[2] The 2009 CIA World Fact Book, "Montserrat."

[3] Ibid.

[4] For general background, see "A Brief History of the Caribbean," by Jan Rogozinski, Penguin Books Ltd., Harmondsworth, England, 2000.. donor countries.

[5] Op cit., CIA World Fact Book.

[6] Op cit., CIA World Fact Book.

7   Op cit., CIA World Fact Book.

Chapter 15-

[1] "Saint Kitts and Nevis," CIA World Fact Book, 2009.
[2] "Saint Kitts and Nevis," Background Notes, US Dept. of Commerce.
[3] Ibid.
[4] "Saint Kitts and Nevis," Wikipedia, March, 2009.
[5] Background Notes, op cit.
[6] A Brief History of the Caribbean, Rogozinski, J., Penguin Books, London UK, 2000. See also: History of the Caribbean, Pons, F. M., Markus Wiener Publishers, Princeton NJ., 2007.
[7] Ibid. See also: Wikipedia.
[8] Background Notes, op cit.
[9] CIA World Fact Book, op cit.
[10] Human Development Indicators, World Bank, 2009.

Chapter 16-

[1] "Saint Lucia," CIA World Fact Book, 2009.
[2] "Saint Lucia," Background Notes, US Dept. of Commerce, 2009.
[3] Ibid.
[4] "Saint Lucia," Wikipedia, March, 2009.
[5] Background Notes, 2009, op cit.
[6] World Development Indicators, World Bank, 2009.
[7] "Saint Lucia," Wikipedia, 2009. See also the following: A Brief History of the Caribbean, Rogozinski, J., Penguin Books, London UK, 2000; History of the Caribbean, Pons, F. M., Markus Wiener Publishers, Princeton NJ.; Background Notes, op cit.
[8] Background Notes, op cit. See also: Wikipedia, 2009.
[9] Ibid. .
[10] Ibid. See also: CIA World Fact Book, 2009.
[11] Corruption Perceptions Index, Transparency International, 2009.
[12] Human Development Report, World Bank, 2009.

Chapter 17-

[1] "Saint Vincent," CIA World Fact Book and Background Notes, 2009.

[2] "Saint Vincent," Background Notes, US Dept. of Commerce, 2009.

[3] Ibid. See also: Wikipedia and World Development Indicators, World Bank, 2009.

[4] "Saint Vincent," Wikipedia, March, 2009. See also the following: A Brief History of the Caribbean, Rogozinski, J., Penguin Books, London UK, 2000; History of the Caribbean, Pons, F. M., Markus Wiener Publishers, Princeton NJ.; Background Notes, op cit.

[5] Ibid.

[6] World Development Indicators, World Bank, 2009. See also: CIA World Fact Book, 2009, and Background Notes, 2009, op cit.

[7] "Saint Vincent," CIA World Fact Book, and Background Notes, op cit.

[8] Human Development Report, World Bank, 2009.

[9] Corruption Perceptions Index, Transparency International, 2009.

Chapter 18-

[1] United States Virgin Islands, Wikipedia (accessed: 19 Sept, 2009).

[2] United States Virgin Islands, Google Maps (accessed: 19 Sept. 2009).

[3] United States Virgin Islands," cia.gov. (accessed: 19 October, 2008)

[4] Ibid.

[5] America's Virgin Islands, Wm. W. Boyer, "Progress and Politics," page 205, Carolina Academic Press, Durham North Carolina, 1983.

[6] Theories about who settled the USVI's first abound and are not terribly important to their current problems. People who had migrated to the islands before the arrivals of the Europeans no longer played a significant role after 1700.

[7] Op cit., America's Virgin Islands, pages 57-58.

[8] Op cit., America's Virgin islands, Chapter 6, "Prejudice and Poverty," pages 110 through 138.

[9] Op cit., America's Virgin Islands, Chapter 8, "Progress and Politics," page 205.

[10] The CIA World Fact Book, Op cit.

[11] Ibid.

[12] Wikipedia, "Political Conditions," Op cit.,

[13] America's Virgin Islands, Op cit., page 205.

[14] Caribbean Net News.com/usvi.php (date accessed: 19 October, 2008.

[15] Ibid.

[16] The World Fact Book, Op cit.

Acknowledgements, Attributions And Credits

1- Central Intelligence Agency 2009 World Fact Book (individual country data on the CIA web site).

2- Background Notes, U.S. Department of Commerce 2009 (individual country data on U.S. Department of Commerce web site).

3- A Brief History of the Caribbean, Rogozinski, Jan, Penguin Books 2000.

4- Modern Latin America, Skidmore, T., Smith, Peter, Oxford University Press, NY 2001.

5- Caribbean Time Bomb, Coram Robert, Wm Morrow & Co, NY 1993.

6- The Last Days of St. Pierre, Zebrowski E., Rutgers Univ. Press, 2002.

7- America's Virgin Islands, Boyer, Wm., Carolina Academic Press, 1983.

8- A History of Barbados, Tree, Ronald, 1972, Random House, 1972.

9- History of the Caribbean, Pons, Frank, Markus Wiener, Publ. 2007.

10- Revolution and Intervention in Grenada, Schoenhals, Kai & Melanson, Richard, Westview Press, 1985.

11- Government and Politics in Africa South of the Sahara, Adam, Thomas,
Random House, NY., 1959.

12- Colonial Policy and Practice, Furnivall, Justin, Cambridge University Press, 1956.

13- Wikipedia.org (for individual country data).

14- Caribbean Net News.com/usvi.php (date accessed: 19 October, 2008).

15- World Development Indicators, World Bank, 2009.

16- Human Development Indicators, World Bank, 2009

17- World Economic Forum, 2009.

18- Transparency International, 2009.

The author also wishes to acknowledge the Fall 2009 semester International Trade class at the Florham campus of Fairleigh Dickinson University, Jillian Griffith and Erika Nies for their copy editing, formatting and data updating assistance.

www.ingramcontent.com/pod-product-compliance
Lightning Source LLC
Chambersburg PA
CBHW031945170526
45157CB00002B/397